Assignments in
Leisure and Tourism

for GNVQ   Book 1

SECOND EDITION

John Ward

The Travel and Tourism Programme

Stanley Thornes (Publishers) Ltd

First published in 1993 by
Stanley Thornes (Publishers) Ltd
Ellenborough House
Wellington Street
Cheltenham GL50 1YW
England

Second edition published in 1996

96 97 98 99 00 / 10 9 8 7 6 5 4 3 2

A catalogue record for this book is available from the British Library.

ISBN 0 7487 2428 1

Typeset by Columns Design and Production Services Ltd, Reading
Printed and bound in Great Britain by Scotprint Ltd, Musselburgh.

Contents

Introduction   v

GNVQ Leisure and Tourism: Unit Summary   x

Acknowledgements   xi

Unit 1: Investigating the leisure and tourism industries

1.1	What is leisure and tourism?	1
1.2	Leisure, tourism and demographic change	2
1.3	Facilities and services provided by the leisure and tourism industries	4
1.4	Leisure and recreation products and services – the role of local authorities	7
1.5	National sports centres	10
1.6	Products/services in the UK travel and tourism industry: English Heritage	13
1.7	The future of tourism in the countryside	17
1.8	Swindon: tourism and the local economy	19
1.9	The social impact of tourism in Calderdale	21
1.10	A new airport – the environmental impact	23

Unit 2: Human resources in the leisure and tourism industries

2.1	Organisation and management at Beaulieu	27
2.2	Teamwork and motivation	30
2.3	Leadership	32
2.4	Conflict and co-operation at work	34
2.5	Games as teamwork training	36
2.6	Teamwork and presenting a good case	39
2.7	Career opportunities	42
2.8	Recruitment and selection procedures: Thomas Cook Retail Travel	44
2.9	Staff appraisal	48
2.10	Visitor attractions: a national code of practice	50
2.11	Company quality assessment schemes	52

Unit 3: Marketing in leisure and tourism

3.1	Pricing decisions in leisure facilities	55
3.2	The role of promotion in marketing leisure facilities	59
3.3	Satisfying the visitor: market research	62
3.4	Marketing tourism: information technology	65
3.5	Marketing *A Day at the Wells*	68
3.6	Beaulieu: marketing an attraction	71
3.7	Marketing national parks	74
3.8	Presenting marketing plans for new products 1	76
3.9	Presenting marketing plans for new products 2	78
3.10	Advertising	80

Unit 4: Finance in the leisure and tourism industries

4.1	Raising finance for projects	83
4.2	Evaluating the financial performance of a guest house	85
4.3	Evaluating the business performance of a leisure park	89
4.4	The National Trust: sources of funding	92
4.5	Financing a tourism business – Dales Cottage Holidays	94
4.6	A business diversifying into tourism: The Teapottery	99
4.7	Preparing a promotional budget for Granada Studios Tour	102
4.8	Managing funds in a professional football club	105

Glossary

| Glossary | 111 |

Introduction

General

This book of assignments has been prepared primarily with the General National Vocational Qualification (GNVQ) in mind, though many of the assignments should prove equally useful to students of other leisure and tourism courses.

One of the main purposes of GNVQs is to provide a national scheme of vocational qualifications which can stand alongside traditional academic qualifications and offer an attractive but rigorous alternative. They are intended to offer a broad-based approach, avoiding a concentration on very narrow vocational skills, which will better equip students either for entry into employment or progression into higher education. Consequently, assignments set on such courses need to be both enjoyable and demanding.

GNVQs are assessed largely on the basis of evidence collected during the course. These assignments are intended to generate a range of outcomes in a variety of forms. Some require student participation in discussion, role play and oral presentation; others demand a variety of written outcomes, including reports, letters, memoranda, diagrams and computer-generated information.

Many of the assignments are structured so that there are some tasks which can be done immediately, these being entirely based on the stimulus material which precedes them. Subsequent tasks will often require discussion and research and are likely to involve co-operative work. The tasks have been designed to generate the kind of evidence required for the cumulative assessment which is central to GNVQ courses.

Level of difficulty

GNVQs are aimed primarily at the 16–19 age group, but the long-term aim is to make them more widely available. Most students are likely to be on full-time school or college courses, in some cases combining GNVQs with GCSE and A or AS level courses.

GNVQs are being developed at three levels of difficulty, with Intermediate and Advanced levels likely to be in most demand in schools and colleges. Achieving a GNVQ at Intermediate level is intended to be the equivalent of taking four GCSE subjects; at Advanced it is intended to represent similar demands to those made on a student taking two A levels, if they complete 12 units, or three A levels if they complete 18. In other words the programmes are intended to appeal to the full ability range and not just to those considered unsuitable for academic courses. The assignments in this book reflect that aim by focusing on complex issues and providing opportunities for the development of a wide range of skills.

The structure of this book is based on the mandatory units required for GNVQ Advanced. Given the considerable overlap in the units at Intermediate and Advanced, however, many of the assignments should prove equally suitable for use at Intermediate level.

The leisure and tourism industry

Leisure and tourism is made up of a wide range of very different, but interdependent, activities and operations. These include accommodation, catering, transport, tourist attractions, sport, entertainment, the arts and other recreation and leisure activities. Its economic importance is proved by the fact that in 1991 tourist expenditure in Britain was around £25 billion. Around 7 per cent of employment in Britain is directly related to tourism.

Though leisure and tourism are growing industries in Britain, they are also changing. For example, traditional longer-stay holidays in British destinations are gradually being replaced by more short breaks, second holidays and day trips. Demand for a range of leisure activities has risen, coinciding with the growing awareness of healthier lifestyles. Forecasts suggest that this growth will continue, but will face strong competition from overseas and especially within the single European market.

The implications of this for future planning suggest that improving quality and value for money is of prime importance and that this can only be achieved by increasing standards of training and professionalism. Vocational qualifications have a part to play in creating a more skilled and knowledgeable work force. Schemes such as the Travel and Tourism Programme, supported by American Express, Forte Hotels, The British Tourist Authority/English Tourist Board, along with Thomas Cook, have shown the industry's commitment to improving knowledge, understanding and skills.

The importance of industry links

Though it is not a requirement that teachers of leisure and tourism GNVQ must have worked at some time in a related occupational area, it is essential that local industry links are established. Students are not required to complete a period of work experience either, but their understanding of the issues facing employees in leisure and tourism are likely to be limited if such links are not established. Students have to know what determines business success, what factors it has to cope with which are outside its control and they have to learn how to develop realistic and viable solutions to practical business problems. The advice and experience of outsiders increases the likelihood that what students are learning reflects practice in the industry itself.

Tutor Guide to the Units in Books 1 and 2

Book 1

Unit 1: Investigating the leisure and tourism industries

By comparison with the other seven mandatory units, Unit 1 covers potentially a vast amount of ground. Its scope makes it important to be selective in providing or suggesting resources. It would be easy to present students with an overwhelming amount of historical and statistical data which might prove discouraging.

Although there is no requirement to approach the units in a specific order, Unit 1 does contain some fundamental issues, an understanding of which is important at the outset. In particular it deals with definitions of leisure and tourism, with the structure and development of both the leisure and recreation industry and the travel and tourism industry, as well as with their social, economic, cultural and environmental impacts.

The assignments reflect the need for students to appreciate the scope and development of leisure and tourism both at national and local levels, as well as ensuring that they also focus on the products and services available through specific facilities.

Unit 2: Human resources in the leisure and tourism industries

This unit combines quite diverse areas of study – organisational structures, teamwork, recruitment and work standards. Some of the assignments reflect theoretical business approaches to issues like organisational structures and teamwork; some show practice in specific working contexts. Given the number of small businesses in leisure and tourism, theory and practice are often quite different!

This unit offers natural links with work undertaken elsewhere in the GNVQ scheme. The assignments which relate to work standards should highlight some general themes which will emerge in more specific contexts in Units 5, 6 and 7. Unit 2 introduces the idea of work standards. Unit 5 should show how they are administered. Unit 6 will demonstrate how customer service is the most important measure of quality for most leisure and tourism businesses. Unit 7 shows the health and safety standards which different sectors of the leisure and tourism industries have to meet.

Unit 3: Marketing in leisure and tourism

This unit focuses on the whole marketing process, from identifying customer needs through to planning promotional campaigns.

The assignments selected reflect the importance of marketing in leisure and tourism. The tasks concentrate mainly on the application of marketing principles in practice. Students have to assess the needs of real customer groups, determine appropriate marketing approaches, design marketing materials, and take account of budgetary target factors.

In most leisure and tourism businesses marketing is firmly controlled by a budget which may well be based on estimates of future performance. However, the process of marketing evaluation is not in practice always regarded as a very exact science. Apart from obvious leaps in sales figures, evaluation may take the form of personal impressions and reports.

Unit 4: Finance in the leisure and tourism industries

This unit stresses the importance to businesses of monitoring their financial performance.

Many students would benefit from an introductory study unit explaining some basic accounting practice and terminology before they have to interpret the data available in company balance sheets and annual reports. Smaller companies are likely to regard data about their financial performance as confidential, but may allow either the use of figures from previous years or figures which have been fictionalised.

The assignments look at the financial issues facing both large organisations, such as the National Trust, and small businesses, such as a family-run guest house.

Book 2

Unit 5: Business systems in the leisure and tourism industries

The complexity and variety of business systems used in the leisure and tourism industries inevitably means students can only become familiar with a representative sample.

The assignments look at systems whose primary functions are related to one of the three elements identified in the unit specification: administration, communications or information-processing. However, it is clear that most business systems combine these functions so that some of the assignments can be easily related to more than one element.

The assignments range in scale from looking at simple paper documentation to complex systems needed to manage a quality standards programme in a national business travel company. Some assignments are based on practice in a specific business context; others, such as the one on telecommunications, demonstrate generally how business systems can be developed.

Unit 6: Developing customer service in leisure and tourism

A high quality of customer service is often regarded as the most vital ingredient in the success of any leisure and tourism business. Many larger organisations use commercially produced customer service training material, such as Welcome Host, but others run their own training programmes, and ideas from some of these are incorporated into the assignments.

Though its importance is undeniable, many of the essential principles of customer service are not particularly complex and are equally important to other industries, most notably retail. The skills involved are often described in very general terms – communication, sales, rapport or efficiency – and these have to be broken down into stages and specific examples. Role plays are particularly useful in showing the relevance of individual skills to particular leisure and tourism contexts.

Unit 7: Health, safety and security in leisure and tourism

Perhaps the best way of bringing health and safety issues to life is to show how they are applied in a range of different workplaces. Hence the assignments cover the health and safety issues ranging from exploring Wookey Hole Caves to firework displays at Alton Towers.

The emphasis on regulation and legislation creates the potential for much very dry reading material. The assignments therefore concentrate on the need for regulation in order to control risks and, where possible, to eliminate hazards. Reference is made only to the most essential clauses of Acts of Parliament or Health and Safety Codes of Practice.

Many of the health, safety and security principles highlighted in this Unit can be applied and evaluated in Unit 8, where students are required to plan and run an event.

Unit 8: Event management

The elements which focus on selecting a viable event and planning it encourage group work and problem-solving and should offer regular opportunities to develop core skills.

The assignments cover extremes of scale, from the national to the local, in order to emphasise both broad planning issues and more specific practical details. It is important that students understand both the planning issues and the practical processes relating to event management.

The assignments provide a foundation for thinking about how to approach the specific events which students will choose to run. Because they are drawn from a range of different locations and are intended to appeal to different audiences, they should also help students to select viable and appropriate events to form the focus of their work for elements 8.2, 8.3 and 8.4.

Combination of units and elements

Each of the 8 units is divided into elements, but student activities are likely to cover more than one element at a time. It is equally possible to plan assignments which cover requirements in more than one unit. Research conducted at a single tourist attraction could provide a range of outcomes. For example, Assignments 2.1 and 3.6 are both based on Beaulieu. Studying a theme, such as the environmental impact of leisure and tourism, would enable students to establish links between Assignments 1.7, 1.10, 2.10, 3.7, 4.4, 6.5, and 7.4. A local study of leisure provision could lead to various combinations of Assignments 1.4, 3.2, 4.3, 5.2, 5.3, 6.10, and 8.3.

Core skills

Three core skills are incorporated into GNVQs: Communication, Application of Number and Information Technology. Like most skills, these are best developed in a realistic context; and they are not therefore isolated in this book but are incorporated within the context of a range of assignments. In other words the skills are used to tackle real problems and issues.

Because of the nature of their content, some units lend themselves particularly to developing individual core skills. Thus Communication is a vital element in Units 2 and 6, since Human Resources and Customer Service are highly dependent on it. Similarly Unit 5, dealing with business systems, is more dependent on Information Technology skills than some others. Assignments featuring Application of Number skills are found in several units but are particularly prominent in Unit 4 where financial issues are covered.

Each assignment is prefaced by an indication of which core skills it might be used to develop.

Active learning

These assignments are intended to encourage students to work both on their own and in small groups. Though resource material is provided, it generally also acts as a starting point for further research. The assignments encourage students to develop planning skills, judgement and initiative. Frequent choices are offered and students may wish to add further appropriate options of their own.

The range of activities

These assignments encourage the production of evidence from students in a variety of forms and from a variety of sources. GNVQs encourage the use of investigations, surveys, case studies and planning and designing activities. This book contains many such practical tasks, providing in many cases source material on which they can be wholly or partly based.

Planning and design tasks include the consideration of posters, notices, floor plans, itineraries, business plans, contingency plans and development proposals. The assignments can be used to generate among other things reports, analyses, speeches or presentations, codes of practice and guidance notes. Responses will be written and oral. Students are challenged to identify a range of principles, qualities, changes, arguments and issues relevant to leisure and tourism. The tasks frequently encourage discussion, in small groups and in role, in order to arrive at consensus or to identify a range of conclusions.

Progression

Since research degrees are awarded for a whole range of leisure and tourism studies, GNVQs provide a number of opportunities for progression. Apart from moving, for example, from Intermediate to Advanced level, successful students can move into higher education to follow diploma or degree courses. In some cases it may be possible to combine these with employment, so that the qualification forms part of the individual's overall training.

Glossary

Definitions and explanations of certain key words and phrases specific to the leisure and tourism industries can be found in the glossary on page 111.

GNVQ Intermediate Leisure and Tourism – unit summary

UNIT 1: INVESTIGATING THE LEISURE AND TOURISM INDUSTRIES (INTERMEDIATE)

Element 1.1: Investigate the leisure and recreation industry nationally and locally

Element 1.2: Investigate the travel and tourism industry nationally and locally

Element 1.3: Prepare for employment in the leisure and tourism industries

UNIT 2: MARKETING AND PROMOTING LEISURE AND TOURISM PRODUCTS (INTERMEDIATE)

Element 2.1: Investigate marketing and promotion in leisure and recreation and travel and tourism organisations

Element 2.2: Plan a leisure and recreation or travel and tourism promotional campaign

Element 2.3: Run and evaluate a leisure or tourism promotional campaign

UNIT 3: CUSTOMER SERVICE IN LEISURE AND TOURISM (INTERMEDIATE)

Element 3.1: Explain the principles of customer service in leisure and tourism

Element 3.2: Investigate the provision of information as part of customer service

Element 3.3: Investigate and demonstrate sales techniques as part of customer service

Element 3.4: Provide and evaluate customer service in leisure and tourism

UNIT 4: CONTRIBUTING TO THE RUNNING OF AN EVENT (INTERMEDIATE)

Element 4.1: Plan an event with others

Element 4.2: Undertake a role in the team event

Element 4.3: Evaluate the team event

GNVQ Advanced Leisure and Tourism – unit summary

UNIT 1: INVESTIGATING THE LEISURE AND TOURISM INDUSTRIES (ADVANCED)

Element 1.1: Investigate the structure and scale of the UK leisure and tourism industries

Element 1.2: Explore the UK leisure and recreation industry and its development

Element 1.3: Explore the UK travel and tourism industry and its development

Element 1.4: Investigate the impact of the UK leisure and tourism industries

UNIT 2: HUMAN RESOURCES IN THE LEISURE AND TOURISM INDUSTRIES (ADVANCED)

Element 2.1: Investigate and compare organisational structures in leisure and tourism

Element 2.2: Investigate how leisure and tourism teams operate

Element 2.3: Investigate, and prepare for, recruitment and selection in leisure and tourism

Element 2.4: Investigate workplace standards and performance in the leisure and tourism industries

UNIT 3: MARKETING IN LEISURE AND TOURISM (ADVANCED)

Element 3.1: Investigate marketing principles, activities and objectives in leisure and tourism

Element 3.2: Analyse and undertake marketing research in leisure and tourism organisations

Element 3.3: Investigate and evaluate marketing communications in leisure and tourism organisations

Element 3.4: Develop a marketing plan for a selected leisure and tourism product/service

UNIT 4: FINANCE IN THE LEISURE AND TOURISM INDUSTRIES (ADVANCED)

Element 4.1: Investigate the financial performance of leisure and tourism organisations

Element 4.2: Examine financial accounts in leisure and tourism organisations

Element 4.3: Investigate and carry out simple budgeting in leisure and tourism

UNIT 5: BUSINESS SYSTEMS IN THE LEISURE AND TOURISM INDUSTRIES (ADVANCED)

Element 5.1: Investigate and evaluate administration systems in leisure and tourism organisations

Element 5.2: Investigate and evaluate communications systems in leisure and tourism organisations

Element 5.3: Investigate and evaluate information-processing systems in leisure and tourism organisations

UNIT 6: DEVELOPING CUSTOMER SERVICE IN LEISURE AND TOURISM (ADVANCED)

Element 6.1: Investigate customer service in leisure and tourism

Element 6.2: Investigate sales and selling as part of customer service in leisure and tourism

Element 6.3: Analyse customer service quality for selected leisure and tourism organisations

Element 6.4: Deliver and evaluate customer service in leisure and tourism organisations

UNIT 7: HEALTH, SAFETY AND SECURITY IN LEISURE AND TOURISM (ADVANCED)

Element 7.1: Investigate health, safety and security in leisure and tourism

Element 7.2: Ensure the health and safety of a leisure and tourism event

Element 7.3: Ensure the security of a leisure and tourism event

UNIT 8 EVENT MANAGEMENT (ADVANCED)

Element 8.1: Propose options and select a feasible event

Element 8.2: Plan an event as a team

Element 8.3: Participate in the running of the team event

Element 8.4: Evaluate individual, team and event performance

Acknowledgements

The author and publishers would like to thank the following organisations for permission to reproduce photographs and other material:

Bath Tourism Marketing (page 2); Thamesdown Leisure Services Department (pages 9–10); English Heritage (page 15); Cumbria Tourist Board (page 18); Architext Publications (page 20); Beaulieu (pages 27, 38); Forte (page 35); Thomas Cook (page 44); The English Tourist Board (page 49, 92); Yorkshire Mining Museum (page 51); Wasps Rugby Football Club (page 62); CNN Marketing Ltd (pages 66–7); A Day at the Wells (page 69); Alton Towers (pages 89, 90); The Teapottery (page 100); Granada Studios Tour (page 104); Swindon Town Football Club (pages 108–9); Tony Stone Images for the cover photograph. All other photographs were supplied by the author.

Every effort has been made to contact copyright holders and we apologise if any have been overlooked.

The Travel and Tourism Programme

An interesting feature of leisure and tourism is its increasing recognition of the importance of education as a means of encouraging young people, teachers and parents to give consideration to what is rapidly becoming the world's largest industrial sector.

Students are being encouraged to view the industries both from the standpoint of discriminating consumers and as career options. With the aim of fostering this dual perspective, the Travel and Tourism Programme, supported by American Express, Forte Hotels, and the British Tourist Authority/English Tourist Board, along with Thomas Cook, has willingly enabled these materials to be written.

John Ward is Programme Development Manager with the Travel and Tourism Programme.

Unit 1 Investigating the leisure and tourism industries

1.1 What is leisure and tourism?

Develops knowledge and understanding of the following element:
1.1   Investigate the structure and scale of the leisure and tourism industry

Supports development of the following core skills:
Application of number 3.1 (Task 1)
Application of number 3.3; Communication 3.3 (Task 2)

A prominent representative of the industry, asked to explain the scope of the leisure and tourism industry, might reply along the following lines:

Tourism is about providing facilities and services that visitors need. This includes all their travel arrangements, their accommodation, what they need to eat and drink, the activities they want to do and the services they need to use during the visit. So it is not surprising to find that leisure and tourism is a complex industry which includes everything from large organisations like international hotel chains and international airlines right down to small operations like souvenir kiosks and independent guides.

It is further complicated by the fact that many parts of the leisure and tourism industry are used by the local community as well as by visitors. Restaurants, public transport, museums and leisure centres provide services which have to meet the needs of both visitors and local residents, whether or not these needs conflict.

Tourism services are provided by both the **public** and **private sectors**, as well as by voluntary organisations. Accommodation is generally owned by private companies, as are many transport services. British Rail is still within the public sector, although there are of course plans to **privatise** it in the near future. Tour operators and travel agents are mainly to be found in the private sector. Perhaps the biggest mixture of ownership is in the area of attractions which may be run by local authorities, public bodies, charitable organisations or commercial companies.

There is an increasing trend for the larger companies involved in leisure and tourism to widen their interests. They may seek to become more international by purchasing interests in overseas companies, as in the case of British Airways' recent interest in other European and American airlines; or they may buy an interest in a leisure and tourism company as a **subsidiary** to their main interest. The well-known brewing company Bass, for example, is also the owner of the Holiday Inn International hotel group. Some companies seek to expand by purchasing an interest in operations which are similar to their own. The Tussauds Group, for example, in addition to the famous waxworks in London, also owns Alton Towers, Chessington World of Adventures, Rock Circus and Warwick Castle.

The leisure and tourism industry in the United Kingdom is more widespread than most of our traditional industries. It is coastal, rural and urban. It includes everything from the countryside pursuits associated with farm-based accommodation to the scientific and industrial centres and museums found in places like Stoke-on-Trent, Ironbridge and Manchester. Our national heritage, in particular our regional history, customs, crafts and architecture, is still able to draw visitors both to traditional historic towns like York and Bath, and also to

Roman Baths Museum Bath: our national heritage is still able to draw visitors to traditional historic sites.

new attractions like The White Cliffs Experience or The Tales of Robin Hood.

I would like to conclude by dispelling a common myth, that the leisure and tourism industry's activities are confined to the summer months. The business traveller, for example, needs services all the year round. Modern working conditions mean that many people have leisure time both at weekends and during the week throughout the whole year. People have always taken day excursions in the autumn and spring, but there has been a major growth in the last few years in the number of people taking short break holidays. A large number of these are associated with special interests, many of which are indoor activities, and there is a growing provision of indoor and all-weather leisure facilities. This means that there are more people who consider taking a break outside the traditional summer season.

Your tasks

1 The above speech is to be made at a conference, but the planners decide that it does not contain sufficient data to support the main points they wish to make.
   Use your own research to produce some figures, statistics and additional examples which could strengthen the impact of the speech.

2 Design and produce a series of four overhead projections (OHPs) which could be used to illustrate the speech effectively.

1.2 Leisure, tourism and demographic change

Develops knowledge and understanding of the following element:
1.1   Investigate the structure and scale of the leisure and tourism industry

Supports development of the following core skills:
Application of number 3.3; Communication 3.1 (Task 1)
Communication 3.1 (Task 2)

Leisure and tourism statistics are important to industry in helping to evaluate people's current habits and predict what they might do in the future. To make even reasonably accurate predictions will often need figures covering a number of years. Sometimes, however, a single year's figures can provide some useful indicators to those involved in the research and planning of new projects in leisure and tourism.

The table below looks at tourism activity in relation to three different ways of dividing the population: by age, by social class, and by the regions in which people live.

Demographic profile of UK tourism in UK 1990

	Total trips	Holiday trips		Visits to friends and relatives non-holiday	Business and work	Adult population of UK
		Short (1–3 nights)	Long (4+ nights)			
Age						
All trips to UK (age 15 and over)	100 %	100 %	100 %	100 %	100 %	100 %
15–24	21	23	13	35	13	20
25–34	22	24	21	20	28	17
35–44	22	23	23	14	29	17
45–54	13	13	12	9	20	13
55–64	11	10	14	9	7	13
65+	11	6	17	13	2	19
Social class						
All trips to UK (age 15 and over)	100 %	100 %	100 %	100 %	100 %	100 %
AB: professional/managerial	30	32	25	27	44	17
C1: clerical/supervisory	27	26	24	31	29	22
C2: skilled manual	25	25	28	23	20	29
DE: unskilled/pensioners, etc.	18	16	23	20	7	32
Region of residence						
All trips to UK (including children)	100 %	100 %	100 %	100 %	100 %	100 %
North	6	8	6	6	6	5
Yorkshire/Humberside	9	10	9	7	6	9
North West	10	9	11	10	10	11
East Midlands	8	8	10	8	7	7
West Midlands	10	10	10	10	9	9
East Anglia	3	2	3	3	4	3
Greater London	12	12	11	15	9	12
South East (excluding Greater London)	20	19	19	20	26	17
South West	9	7	8	12	11	8
Scotland	5	6	7	3	5	9
Wales	5	5	5	6	6	5
Northern Ireland	2	3	2	1	1	4

Based on the characteristics of UK resident adults who formed the basis of the sample survey.

1 Discuss what conclusions each of the following five individuals might reach after they had studied the table on page 3 carefully:

  a) the Marketing Manager of the Yorkshire and Humberside Tourist Board

  b) the developers of a business and conference centre planned for a site in the East Midlands region

  c) a new tour operator planning to specialise in coach trips for the over-60s

  d) a hotel manager based in East Anglia intending to market a new weekend break offer

  e) a research student writing a thesis on the subject of 'Transport, mobility and the extended family'.

2 Use published data to help you to compile a list of the most significant demographic changes in the United Kingdom in the last 20 years.
  Discuss the extent to which you think each of these changes has affected the following:
  ● local authority leisure provision
  ● the development of regional tourist attractions
  ● the marketing of specific overseas destinations.

1.3 Facilities and services provided by the leisure and tourism industries

Develops knowledge and understanding of the following element:
1.1 Investigate the structure and scale of the UK leisure and tourism industries

Supports development of the following core skills:
Communication 3.2 (Task 1)
Communication 3.2, 3.4 (Task 2)
Communication 3.2, 3.3; Information Technology 3.3, 3.4 (Task 3)

What sort of facilities and services do tourists need?

In addition to requiring accommodation, transport systems and attractions, tourists also have other needs. Before departure they may need to make financial arrangements involving currency exchange or travellers cheques. Most will invest in some kind of insurance against injury or other disruption to their travels. Once they have arrived in their chosen destination they will need facilities like banks, shops and restaurants. They may also use leisure facilities such as swimming pools or tennis courts. If it is their first visit they will probably call on the services of a **Tourist Information Centre** to find out the most interesting places to visit. They may also take advantage of the services of local guides or of coaches qualified to teach skills such as canoeing or windsurfing.

What is the difference between a facility and a service?

It is not always easy to distinguish between a facility and a service. A service is generally something which someone does for you; a facility is a place provided for a specific use. The terms can be defined as follows:

- *a service* provides actions on an organised commercial basis which meet someone else's needs, e.g. home delivery pizzas
- *a facility* is something specially arranged or constructed in order to provide either recreation or a service, e.g. a restaurant.

Many tourist attractions provide a mixture of services and facilities in order to meet the varied needs of their visitors. The list below indicates what is available at the National Trust property, Fountains Abbey:

Disabled visitors
- Minibus to Abbey
- Powered runarounds and wheelchairs
- Adapted WC available
- Level access to Abbey grounds and visitor centre
- Guided tours for visually impaired people

Families
- Baby rooms
- High chairs and children's menu
- Activities programme

Educational
- Resource book for teachers
- Education Officer

Some of the items on this list, such as the guided tours, would be classified as services, while others, such as the baby rooms, are more likely to be described as facilities.

How destinations list their services and facilities

As the Fountains Abbey list shows, destinations and attractions do not always make a clear distinction between services and facilities. Blackpool, the most popular of all British seaside resorts, provides a variety of information for the travel trade, in which it lists all of the following as local services:

- late night petrol stations
- audio-visual suppliers
- car hire
- coach and car parks
- currency exchange
- holiday associations
- tourist information centres
- markets
- postal and telephone information
- local newspapers
- radio stations
- taxis
- theatres
- cabaret shows
- theatre booking agencies
- police
- hospitals

Other destinations list the following as local facilities:

- theatres
- cinemas
- museums
- shops
- sports facilities
- water and winter sports
- caravan sites

Clearly there is some overlap between what is described as a facility and what is called a service. Since the term 'facilities' is often applied to buildings constructed to provide recreation or service, it includes both individual attractions and accommodation. In other words, although they are both buildings, museums may be listed as facilities because they are regarded as attractions; caravan sites may be listed as services because they provide accommodation.

The services and facilities to be found in a single destination will reflect both its history, and how keen local residents and politicians are to attract more visitors. The following description of Hartlepool shows how a coastal town has used its maritime history to develop facilities which have increased the number of visitors to the town.

Hartlepool . . . history in the making

As with many coastal towns, much interest and activity centres around the sea front and harbours. Hartlepool is no exception and where, a short time ago you would have found shipyards, today you can experience one of the most exciting marina developments on the east coast.

The initial berthing provision for 80 boats was immediately doubled to 160 to meet the demand for first class facilities. Over 750 berths will be provided, making Hartlepool the largest and finest marina in the North.

It is here that you will find the HMS Trincomalee and the paddle steamer Wingfield Castle. The latter, having spent her life ferrying passengers across the River Humber, is now open to the public along with Trincomalee, built in 1817, and the world's second oldest floating warship. See for yourself the dedication and painstaking skill that is needed to rebuild a ship of such character.

For sailing enthusiasts, whether you choose to take part or merely watch from dry land, the Tees Sailing Club organises both dinghy and yacht racing, while Hartlepool's Yacht Club is ideally situated for yachting, windsurfing and waterskiing.

Hartlepool is one of the few east coast towns to sustain a thriving fishing industry. Sea angling championships are held annually and many of the local fishing boats are licensed to take out fishing parties.

For those who are fond of shopping, the town centre boasts the recently refurbished Middleton Grange Centre. You'll also discover one of the area's best open markets together with a bric-a-brac and antique market.

For sporting enthusiasts Hartlepool has plenty to offer: from the Mill House Leisure Centre and swimming pool to its well supported football club and three rugby union clubs. There is a ten pin bowling centre as well as flat green bowling and an 18-hole golf course overlooking the sea.

Music is very much part of the town's culture and if you enjoy listening to band concerts, take a stroll into Ward Jackson Park where, in the summer months, traditional bands entertain from a beautifully restored bandstand. This park is just one of five in the area which together provide playgrounds, boating lakes, putting greens and tennis courts, as well as peaceful walks and splendid flower displays.

You will find a visit to Hartlepool's 'Generations of Energy' exhibition both enthralling and stimulating. The award winning show provides a 'hands on' live exhibition that explores how different *forms of electricity are generated and their effect on our environment. The Centre welcomes visitors and its friendly, helpful staff are available to answer all your questions.*

Your tasks

1 List the facilities mentioned in the description of Hartlepool and describe the main categories of visitors you think the town would appeal to.

2 Refer to Assignment 1.4 for a brief description of the roles of the public, private and voluntary sectors in the provision of leisure and tourism facilities. Suggest three services or facilities in Hartlepool which representatives from each of these sectors might have a role in developing, in order to attract more of the categories of visitors you identified in task 1.

3 Information is a vital service for tourists. Make a list of all the questions a first-time visitor to a destination might ask. Identify the different methods by which information can be communicated to visitors. Suggest which would be the most appropriate method of answering each of the questions and explain why. Investigate the provision of tourist information in a specific destination in order to determine the relative parts played by the different sectors in providing it.

1.4 Leisure and recreation products and services – the role of local authorities

Develops knowledge and understanding of the following element:
1.2   Explore the UK leisure and recreation industry and its development

Supports development of the following core skills:
Communication 3.2, 3.4 (Task 1)
Communication 3.2, 3.4 (Task 2)
Communication 3.2 (Task 3)

People choose how to spend their leisure time from a wide range of activities. Some of these, like reading or watching television, can be done at home. Others, like watching a football match, learning to paint or going to the cinema, depend on suitable facilities being available. The most popular leisure activities which people take part in outside their homes include:
- eating out at restaurants
- participating in and watching sporting events
- attending plays and music concerts
- going to the cinema
- going to public houses
- gambling.

The facilities needed to enable people to pursue these activities are provided by organisations from all sectors of the economy. The **public sector**, mainly through local government, often provides facilities such as parks and swimming pools. The **private sector**, through commercial enterprises such as golf clubs or cinemas, also provides leisure facilities. The **voluntary sector** is also involved through organisations like amateur sports clubs and drama societies. There is also an increasing trend for facilities to be developed and managed through partnerships between the public and private sectors.

The table below offers some examples of facilities which are commonly, though not always, mainly identified with either the public, private or voluntary sectors:

Sector	Interests within sector	Examples of provision
Public sector	Central government	Royal parks, national sports centres, e.g Lilleshall, Bisham Abbey
	Local government	Playing fields, swimming pools, leisure centres, parks, gardens, allotments, community centres, libraries, regional theatres
Private sector	Members' only sports clubs	Golf, squash, snooker, health and fitness centres, country clubs
	Payment on admission entertainment centres	Cinemas, theatres, bowling alleys, skating rinks, dance halls, professional sport, theme parks, bingo halls
	Employee benefits	Company-owned sports grounds, bars, dance and entertainment venues
Voluntary sector	Amateur sports clubs and arts groups	Amateur drama/opera groups, hockey, rugby, cricket and soccer clubs
	Interest groups and charities	Conservation and heritage groups, community action groups, youth organisations

Thamesdown Leisure Services Department

Thamesdown is a local authority providing leisure services for a population of around 176,000. Its leisure services department is divided into four sections:
- *Recreation* – including leisure centres, golf courses and outdoor sport
- *Arts and Museums* – including management of Lydiard House and the Wyvern Theatre
- *Landscape and Countryside* – including parks, allotments and children's play areas
- *Client Services* – including marketing, accounts and administration.

The range of facilities run by the council includes indoor sports centres, swimming pools, playing fields, arts centres, a museum and art gallery, a theatre, a railway museum and two country parks.

The leisure services department has a net budget of £11 million after turnover. From this they aim both to meet the leisure and recreational needs of the people of Swindon, and also to help to develop Swindon as an attractive location in which to live. This second purpose is part of a process of trying to attract new business and industry to the area. All of the facilities within the recreation division are managed on six-year contracts which were opened to compulsory competitive tendering in 1992. All the contracts were won by in-house teams.

The ability of local authorities to provide new facilities or upgrade existing ones is dependent on the funds they have available. Central government imposes restrictions on local government spending, an important factor since authorities like Thamesdown receive funds to pay for leisure facilities from council tax. At present Thamesdown Council is only allowed to use 20 per cent of its receipts from council tax on new projects. Other income comes from admission fees, some sponsorship, and from grants from organisations like the Sports Council, the Arts Council, the Forestry Commission and the Countryside Commission. In all these grants totalled £400,000 in 1993.

Meeting local demand for leisure facilities and services requires Thamesdown Leisure Services to employ the equivalent of 450 full-time staff. This includes a range of jobs, such as landscape gardeners, managers and administrators, receptionists, engineers, fitness trainers, lifeguards and cleaners. Though different skills and qualifications are required for different jobs, Thamesdown Leisure Services provides work training schemes for all new employees.

Leisure facilities cost money to run all the time they are open. Staff have to be paid, heating and light has to be provided, and equipment and the fabric of the buildings has to be maintained. However, they are in general much more heavily used at weekends and in the early evening, times when potential users are less likely to be committed to work or other duties. In order to encourage use at quieter times, Thamesdown Leisure Services runs a Gold Card scheme. Members of the scheme must either be receivers of State benefit in some form or be senior citizens. Nine thousand of the scheme's 17,000 members are senior citizens. Membership provides cheap admission to facilities during off peak hours.

Your tasks

Study the timetable of events offered by the Parks and Countryside section of Thamesdown Leisure Services Department for October 1994.

October

Saturday 8th October   10.00 am or 2.00 pm
WINTER HANGING BASKETS
Make a basket of colourful winter flowering pansies.
All materials provided.
Meet: The Community Garden Centre
Cheney Manor Industrial Estate
Cost: £14.00
PLEASE BOOK IN ADVANCE
ON (01793) 523294

Sunday 9th October   10.30 am
MILLING AROUND WROUGHTON
Discover how to reach Wroughton from Coate Water on $8\frac{1}{2}$ mile circular walk. We'll be stopping for lunch at a local pub and continuing on to find out about Wroughton's past.
Meet: Coate Water Country Park Ranger's Cottage
Cost: Adults £2.00   Juniors £1.00
PLEASE BOOK IN ADVANCE
ON (01793) 490150
Dogs welcome, please wear stout footwear

Saturday 15th October 10.00 am or 2.00 pm
WINTER HANGING BASKET
Create an "Evergreen" basket with a selection of Ivies and other green or variegates plants to maintain interest through the winter.
All materials provided.
Meet: The Community Garden Centre
Cheney Manor Industrial Estate
Cost: £14.00
PLEASE BOOK IN ADVANCE
ON (01793) 490150

Saturday 15th October   2.00 pm
FUNGUS FOR FOOD?
Learn how to identify some of our local mushrooms at Coate Water. We'll be tasting some of the edible ones and learning really wild recipes.
Meet: Coate Water Country Park Ranger's Cottage
Cost: Adults £3.00   Juniors £1.50
PLEASE BOOK IN ADVANCE
Continued

9

24th – 30th October   10.00 am every day
SNAPPY SKETCHING COMPETITION
A sketching event for children under 16. Come along and sketch your favourite photograph from our 'captured' exhibition.
Prize awarded for winning entry.
Pens and Paper provided.
Meet: Lydiard Country Park visitor Centre
Cost: 50p
Entries will be judged on the 30th at 12.00 midday.

24th October – 4th November
'CAPTURED'
A photographic exhibition of work by a local photographer showing landscapes and skyscapes of Lydiard Country Park.
Meet: Lydiard Country Park Visitor Centre
Free

Thursday 27th October   10.00 am
MUSICAL MADNESS
A workshop event for youngsters, making musical rhythmical instruments from natural materials. Finishing off with a performance to be recorded live!
Meet: Lydiard Country Park Visitors Centre
Cost: £1.00

Saturday 29th October   1.30 pm
AN EARTHWALK
We'll be exploring nature in a very different way on this Saturday, walking in the treetops and crawling in the leafmould might give you some ideas.
Meet: Coate Water Country Park Ranger's Cottage
Cost: £1.00
PLEASE BOOK IN ADVANCE
ON (01793) 490150
Please wear old clothes.

October–April.   1st Sunday of every month 10.00 am
COPPICING SKILLS
Try your hand at this ancient skill in Peatmoor Woodland. You will learn how to coppice trees and how your days work will improve the area for wildlife.
Bring old clothes and a packed lunch.
Meet: Peatmoor Community Woodland Whitefield Crescent, off Swinley Drive, off Peatmoor Way

---

1 Identify which groups of people you think each event is intended to appeal to.

2 List the factors which you think might have influenced the type of events being offered.

3 Suggest other events Thamesdown Leisure Services Department might provide at these three facilities which might appeal to a wider audience.

1.5 National sports centres

Develops knowledge and understanding of the following element:
1.2 Explore the UK leisure and recreation industry and its development

Supports development of the following core skills:
Communication 3.4 (Task 1)
Communication 3.4 (Task 2)
Communication 3.4 (Task 3)
Communication 3.2 (Task 4)
Communication 3.2 (Task 5)

Participation in sport is an important part of many people's lives. National government tries to encourage this in a number of ways. It does not fund the building of facilities directly, but it does contribute, through a grant from the Department of National Heritage, to the finances of organisations like the Sports Council. The main objectives of the Sports Council are:

1   to encourage more people to take part in sport
2   to increase the number and quality of available sports facilities
3   to improve standards of sports performance
4   to provide data and information about sport in the UK.

The Sports Council is involved in promoting sports participation at all levels, whether it be by ordinary members of the community or by people who are particularly talented at sport. In order to encourage the development of special skills, five national centres have been set up. The Sports Council is responsible for the general management of these centres, though their day-to-day running is handled by private contractors.

These five centres provide facilities, accommodation and environments for developing sporting excellence. Each centre provides a specialist range of facilities, equipment and expertise, and is used mainly by the governing bodies of different sports. For example the Football Association may use the Lilleshall Centre as a base for training activities for regional representative teams or national squads of players. However, specialist facilities at these national centres can also be hired by individuals or groups to pursue activities like squash, climbing, tennis or rowing.

The national centres derive additional income through the provision of conference centres and through the development of courses designed to meet the specific needs of different interest groups. They are ideally placed to offer conference facilities, since they combine pleasant settings with residential and sports facilities.

The five National Centres are as follows.

Bisham Abbey
A major indoor facility sited in a 12th-century abbey on the edge of the River Thames. Contains extensive artificial playing surfaces
Main sports catered for
Tennis, soccer, hockey, squash, weight training, golf
Accommodation
Available for 29 people in the Abbey and a further 51 in a recently completed block
Catering facilities
A dining hall and private function rooms in the Abbey, and a licensed bar in the new block
Conference facilities
The Elizabethan Room seats 90, but a variety of smaller well- equipped conference rooms are also available
Location
Approximately one hour's drive from London and 17 miles from Heathrow Airport – close to Marlow in Buckinghamshire

Crystal Palace
A large multi-purpose sports facility incorporating a stadium, a swimming pool, and a variety of indoor facilities and artificial surfaces
Main sports catered for
Athletics, swimming, boxing, martial arts, judo and basketball

Accommodation
A modern building within the grounds accommodates up to 135 people
Catering facilities
A self-service restaurant is available and a range of catering services can be arranged for special events
Conference facilities
Up to 150 delegates can be accommodated in the largest hall; smaller conference rooms and lecture rooms are also available
Location
In London, very close to Crystal Palace railway station which has a regular service to Victoria, and close to the South Circular Road

Lilleshall
A multi-purpose centre based around a former hunting lodge. The grounds include tennis courts, playing fields, various artificial surfaces and a range of indoor facilities
Main sports catered for
Soccer, table tennis, cricket, gymnastics, archery, hockey and golf
Accommodation
108 modern rooms able to accommodate up to 180 people
Catering facilities
A dining area offering both cafeteria-style meals and full service menus
Conference facilities
A lecture theatre holding up to 180 delegates is supported by a variety of smaller conference rooms
Location
12 miles off the M6 in Shropshire; within easy reach of Wolverhampton, Shrewsbury and Stafford

Holme Pierrepont
A water sports centre set in parkland adjacent to the River Trent, with a lake, ski tow ropes and canoe slalom
Main sports catered for
Rowing, canoeing, water skiing, windsurfing, sailing and fishing
Accommodation
Modern rooms available for up to 66 guests
Catering facilities
A cafeteria-style dining room and also rooms available for private functions
Conference facilities
A lecture room with space for 170 delegates and several smaller rooms – exhibition space also available
Location
A rural setting approximately 3-and-a-half miles from Nottingham city centre

Plas Y Brenin
A major centre, based in former hotel premises, for mountain activities, with access to excellent rock climbing, as well as lakes, rivers and forests
Main sports catered for
Mountain climbing, rock climbing, canoeing, orienteering, dry slope skiing

Accommodation
Basic accommodation for 70 people and additional self-catering facilities for a further 16 people
Catering facilities
A dining room offers a variety of menus
Conference facilities
A lecture room accommodating up to 95 people, supported by a smaller room taking up to 15 people
Location
On the A4086 in Snowdonia, just off the A5 London to Holyhead road

Your tasks

1 List reasons why you think national governments might wish to encourage the development of sporting excellence.

2 What problems do governments face in ensuring that facilities to promote sporting excellence are available to people in all regions of the UK?

3 What factors do you think were taken into consideration in deciding which sports each of the National Centres should cater for?

4 Choose one of the five National Centres, and research the feasibility of its access and use by parties of school or college students.

5 Choose a suitable location for the development of a sixth National Centre. Write a report indicating:

   a) the reasons for your choice of location

   b) the range of sports you think it should cater for and why

   c) the specialist facilities which should form part of the development

   d) the factors which would make the inclusion of these specialist facilities more or less acceptable both to funders and to those responsible for granting planning permission.

1.6 Products/services in the UK travel and tourism industry: English Heritage

Develops knowledge and understanding of the following element:
1.3   Explore the UK travel and tourism industry and its development

Supports development of the following core skills:
Communication 3.4 (Task 1)
Communication 3.2 (Task 2)
Communication 3.2, 3.3 (Task 3)
Application of number 3.2 (Task4)

English Heritage is an independent organisation with a major responsibility for heritage conservation. In addition to raising money from membership, admission charges to properties and running special events, English Heritage receives government funding from the Department of National Heritage in order to support its work.

The main activities of English Heritage are:
- conservation of the historic environment
- funding rescue archaeology
- funding support to conservation areas
- funding repairs to historic buildings and ancient monuments.

English Heritage is providing a major general service to the public, both in restoring historic sites and in making them accessible for the public to visit. However, individual English Heritage sites also offer a range of products and services, most with the added advantage for the organisation of generating extra revenue. These services include:

Special events	– re-enactments of battles and historic events
	– musical performances
	– plays
Concerts	– open air concerts
	– operas
	– concert recitals
	– pop concerts
Retailing	– souvenir shops
	– book shops
	– self-selection shops selling wider range of goods
Catering	– restaurants, tea rooms and cafes
	– outlets selling ice-creams and soft drinks
Information and interpretation	– explanatory graphics
	– audio tours
	– exhibitions
	– handbooks and guides
	– interactive video
	– tape tours for disabled people
Foreign languages	– foreign language booklets and guides
	– foreign language audio tours
	– translations of site graphics and exhibition panels
	– foreign language promotional material
	– multi-lingual phrase and vocabulary information for custody staff
Education services	– published resources for teachers
	– videos and publications to support the National Curriculum
	– free visits for educational visitors.

English Heritage has invested a lot of time in developing its education services. Free teachers' information sheets are available at most sites, and free exploratory visits by teachers and lecturers are also encouraged. Some sites have an education centre with resources relating to the site and its history available for study.

Education officers are provided at some sites to give advice and information. A free magazine, *Heritage Learning*, is published three times a year. It suggests a number of practical activities, focusing on heritage sites, which can be used to bring the curriculum to life. Visits to heritage sites are an obvious means of bringing history lessons to life, but they can also be used to develop practical activities in subjects like geography, science and English.

The list of educational resources produced by English Heritage is extensive. It includes books, videos, posters, slide packs and computer software. Teachers' handbooks cover over 40 of English Heritage's historic properties. These include historical background, documentary sources and activity sheets, for use both in the classroom and during site visits.

Extract from English Heritage guide to free educational visits 1995–6.

ADVANCED BOOKING ESSENTIAL

Educational visits to the sites in this section must be pre-booked at least 14 days in advance. At some of these sites prior arrangement is necessary, to get a key for instance.

SOUTH WEST

English Heritage, Historic Properties South West, 7/8 King Street, Bristol BS1 4EQ.
Tel: 0117-975 0719
Fax 0117-975 0701
Avon, Berkshire, Cornwall, Devon, Dorset, Gloucestershire, Isles of Scilly, Oxfordshire, Somerset, Wiltshire (except Stonehenge).

CORNWALL

Chysauster Ancient Village ㅠ
A deserted Romano-Cornish village with a 'street' of eight well preserved houses, each comprising a number of rooms around an open court.
2¹/₂m NW of Gulval off B3311.

Launceston Castle ♜
Set on the motte of the original Norman castle and commanding the town and surrounding countryside, the shell keep and tower survive of this medieval castle which controlled the main route into Cornwall.
In Launceston.

Pendennis Castle ♜ 🏛 ♥
Erected by Henry VIII, well preserved granite gun fort and outer ramparts with great angled bastions defended against invasion from the sea. The site is an excellent base for studying coastal defence.
On Pendennis Head, 1m SE of Falmouth.

Restormel Castle ♜
Perched on a high mound, surrounded by a deep moat, the huge circular keep of this splendid Norman castle survives in remarkably good condition.
1¹/₂m N of Lostwithiel off A390.

St Mawes Castle ♜ ♣
Built by Henry VIII to guard the entrance to safe anchorage in the Carrick Roads, its three huge circular bastions with gun ports were formidable defences indeed.
In St Mawes on A3078.

Tintagel Castle ♜
The spectacular setting for the legendary castle of King Arthur. Clinging to the edge of the cliff face are the extensive

Pendennis Castle, Cornwall.

ruins of a medieval royal castle built by Richard, Earl of Cornwall.
On Tintagel Head, ¹/₂m along uneven track from Tintagel, no vehicles.

KEY TO SYMBOLS

Types of building or monument
✝ Abbey and other ecclesiastical building
♣ Garden
🏛 Historic House
⌐ Industrial monument, bridge, farm building or other post-medieval monument
♜ Medieval castle, site or later fortification
ㅠ Prehistoric site
♨ Roman site

Facilities and resources
🏛 Education Centre
♥ Teacher's handbook
▭▭ Video

English Heritage provides a comprehensive guide for teachers planning a site visit. This gives details of individual properties, indicating their locations, opening times, main points of interest and whether or not visits to them need to be booked in advance.

The sites which have education centres provide equipment and resources for specific use during educational visits. This generally falls into four categories:

Practical equipment
    – tapes for making measured drawings
    – binoculars for close observation
    – clip boards for note making and sketches 'on the move'

Primary sources	– maps
	– plans
	– documents
	– archive photographs and engravings
	– books
Projectors, slides and videos	– slide projectors and slide sets
	– VCR and video tapes about different aspects of the site and the role of English Heritage
Handling material	– archaeological finds
	– model room sets with costume figures
	– Victorian toys
	– replica costumes for trying on.

Your tasks

Read the following account of the products and services available at English Heritage sites for foreign language speakers:

English Heritage has recognised the need to develop its foreign language provision and is doing what it can, within funding constraints. A total of 33 foreign language publications has been produced, including:
- *Stonehenge souvenir guides (French, German)*
- *brief guides in French, German, Japanese, Spanish, Italian and Dutch*
- *foreign language audio tours at nine properties*

These have mainly been produced for properties such as Dover Castle or Stonehenge, with an obvious need, or where local enthusiasts have provided suitable texts.

Site graphics and exhibition panels have been translated into other languages as at Battle Abbey. Promotional material has been produced and widely distributed in French, German and Japanese, Italian and Spanish.

Efforts have been made to encourage custody staff to develop language skills. A multi-lingual desk mat giving common phrases and historic monument specific vocabulary (e.g. tower, crenellation) with accompanying audio tape has been circulated to properties.

1 Either arrange to visit a site of historic interest in the company of a non-English speaker or, if you have the opportunity while on holiday, visit a similar site yourself in a country where the language is not familiar to you.

2 Note any difficulties which arise in understanding what the site contains or what its significance is.

3 Propose three products or services which would enable foreign-language speakers to gain a better appreciation of their visit.

4 Assess the economic and practical factors which would render each of your three proposals viable or otherwise.

1.7 The future of tourism in the countryside

Develops knowledge and understanding of the following element:
1.2 Explore the UK leisure and recreation industry and its development

Supports development of the following core skills:
Communication 3.1, 3.2 (Task 1)
Communication 3.4 (Task 2)

Many modern tourists are motivated by a strong need to escape from the urban environment. However, as greater numbers are drawn towards the most attractive landscapes, the quality and accessibility of the countryside come under threat. There is a great problem in trying to reconcile the need for leisure activity and the need to conserve the countryside. This is what the Countryside Commission has to say on the subject:

Providing facilities, such as car parks, toilets and shelter, for visitors to the countryside is often a costly task for recreation providers. Tourism operators could assist by allowing their own facilities to be used by a wider clientele beyond their existing customers. Such dual use of facilities would be a more effective use of resources and would be of mutual benefit because it would enhance the image of tourism businesses among potential future customers.

The Commission looks to the tourism industry to take the initiative in channelling some of its profits and visitor spending towards countryside conservation and recreation work. The Commission will assist by giving general advice on the most appropriate mechanisms and, in major schemes, will assist in the identification of projects and conservation organisations most able to carry out the work.

In addition, the contact that tourism businesses and their staff have with visitors means that they are well-placed to promote the values of conservation and considerate conduct among their guests, which is so important for the harmonious relationship between tourism and the environment. Studies have shown, however, that the contents of tourism literature often fail to give the visitor a better understanding or appreciation of the area promoted.

Here is a challenge: the creative and marketing talents of the tourism industry could be used to great effect in supporting conservation and sustainable tourism use of the countryside.

The national network of **Tourism Information Centres** has great potential for acting as a much-needed focus for information on the countryside. Developing this potential would improve their usefulness to local people and tourists, alike.

Policies for tourism should be:
- the tourism industry should use its marketing activities, particularly leaflets and brochures, to stimulate a greater sense of care and understanding among visitors about the places they visit
- tourism operators should share their facilities more widely with visitors to the countryside
- the tourism industry should set up environmental funds, and other mechanisms, for attracting resources from visitors and tourism businesses into practical conservation and recreation work
- the development of tourism in the countryside should follow the Principles for Tourism in the Countryside endorsed by the Commission and the **English Tourist Board**.

Rydal Water, Cumbria.

Your tasks

1   Draw up your own list of principles or guidelines which you think should apply to the further development of tourism in the countryside.

   Compare your own list with the suggestions made by others in the group and try to establish which ones you all agree on. Arrange these under a series of major headings. How do your ideas compare with those suggested by the English Tourist Board and The Countryside Commission in the extract quoted here?

2   Choose a countryside location which is known to appeal to tourists. Collect a selection of brochures and leaflets which promote its various attractions and which illustrate the range of facilities and services available.

   Study this tourist literature and evaluate it from two points of view:

   a)   How effectively does it give the visitor an understanding of the area promoted?

   b)   Does it contribute in any way to the conservation of the area?

3   Write a report summarising how the literature could contribute more to making sure that the area keeps its attractiveness.

1.8 Swindon: tourism and the local economy

Develops knowledge and understanding of the following element:
1.4 Investigate the impact of the UK leisure and tourism industries

Supports development of the following core skills:
Communication 3.1, 3.4 (Task 1)
Communication 3.2, 3.4 (Task 2)

We have long been used to brochures and advertisements praising the merits of seaside resorts and rural beauty spots, but now less obvious tourist destinations are beginning to seek greater economic benefit from tourism. A good example is Swindon, for many years known mainly as a railway town. The following extract introduces the town's Visitors' Guide:

Swindon offers you the best of both worlds: a wide choice of town and country attractions, combining all the benefits of a 'city break' with the chance to explore rural England at its most appealing.

Despite its young and modern image, Swindon is not a new town. For nearly 150 years it was one of the world's great railway centres. Today you can savour the heritage of Brunel's Great Western Railway at the Railway Museum and the unique Railway Village, one of the earliest and most perfect examples of a planned workers' estate. In the Old Town there is an even earlier Swindon to be discovered. Many fine buildings recall the original hill-top market town which was mentioned in the Domesday Book. At its heart is The Lawn, a 50-acre park which was the home of the Goddard family, Swindon's 'Lords of the Manor' for over 300 years. In sharp contrast, Swindon's new business parks provide some celebrated examples of contemporary architecture – striking symbols of Swindon's place at the forefront of the hi-tech revolution.

Superb leisure facilities mean Swindon is great for families. The exciting Domebusters water-slides at the Oasis, ice-skating at the Link Centre, ten-pin bowling at the Superbowl or the latest movies at the 7-screen cinema will all keep the children happy while you can take time to explore one of the many historic houses nearby or enjoy a leisurely cream tea. Top class evening entertainment is provided at the Wyvern Theatre and the Town's other arts venues, while a wide range of restaurants and nightclubs cater for all ages and tastes.

Less than an hour from London by High Speed Train and easily accessible from all parts of Britain, Swindon is at the centre of England's finest countryside and most famous attractions. Whether for a short break or a longer holiday, Swindon has all the ingredients you need: touring, walking, sporting, cycling, living it up or just winding down!

Your tasks

1 Use a good road atlas to locate tourist attractions within easy reach of Swindon and the main access routes to them. You might include the following: Bath, the Vale of the White Horse at Uffington, Avebury Stone Circle, the Railway Centre at Didcot, the Thames Valley, the Kennet and Avon Canal, the Cotswolds, Oxford.

Discuss the numbers and type of visitors each of these locations might attract, how much economic benefit the local community is likely to gain from these visits, and whether their nearness to Swindon is an overall advantage or disadvantage to those trying to market Swindon as a tourist attraction.

2 Read the following information about how to get to Swindon and then study the map below.

- **Road:** Swindon is served by the M4 motorway, Junctions 15 (East) and 16 (West) and the A4361, A361, A420, A345, and A419 trunk roads. London is only 90 minutes by road, Bristol 40 minutes. Regular National Express coach services run from London and other major towns and cities

- **Air:** from London Heathrow it is quicker to reach Swindon than Central London itself! The M4 provides a direct route from Heathrow, while rail travellers can take

Swindon town centre.

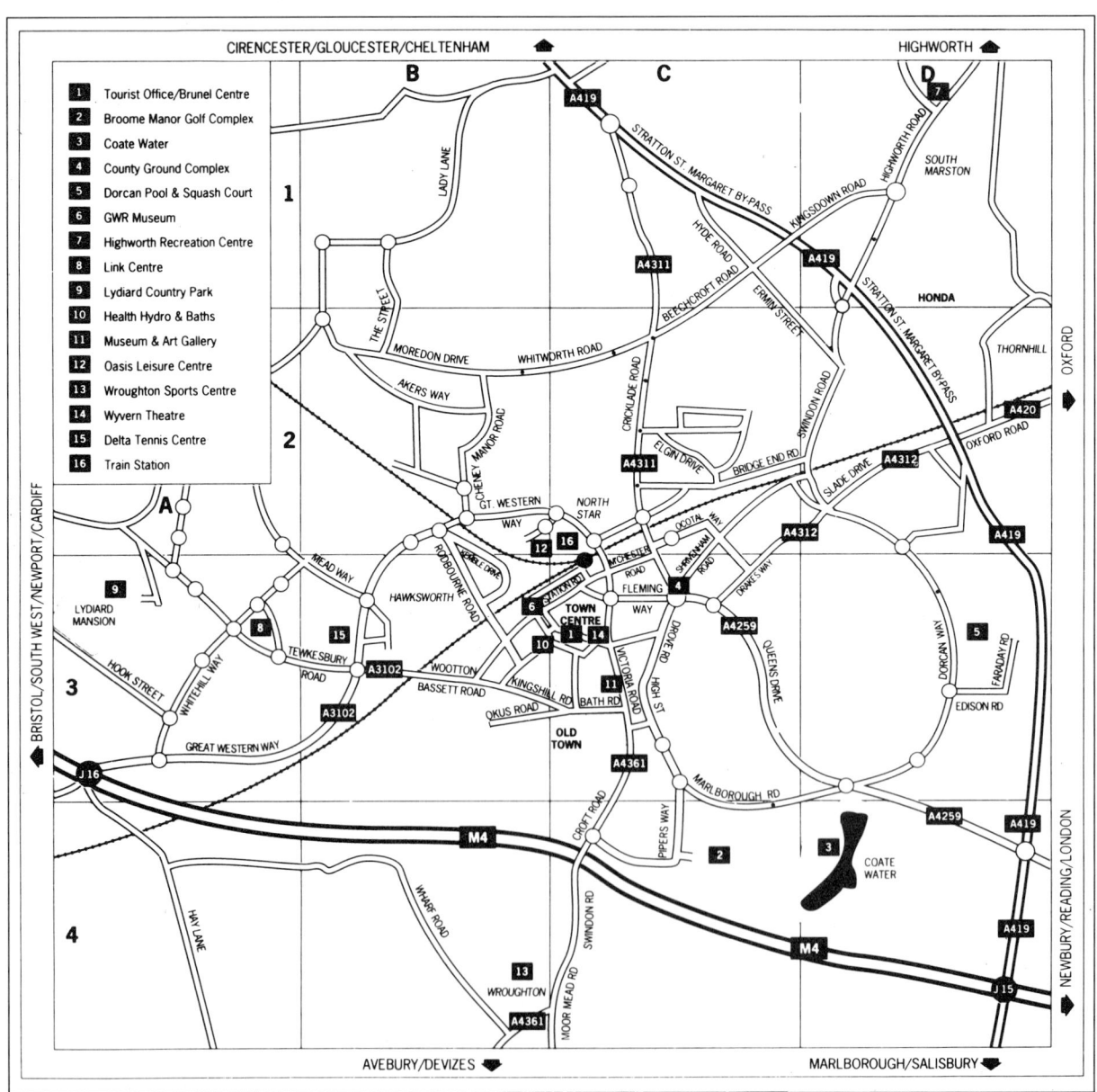

a fast coach to Reading to connect with a High Speed Train. From Gatwick the M25 connects with the M4, while Bristol, Cardiff and Southampton airports are all within easy reach

- **Rail:** Swindon is only 50 minutes from London by High Speed Train. The 125 service also links Swindon with Bath, Bristol, and South Wales, while other services provide easy access to the Midlands and North.

Find two kinds of leisure or tourism provision which the town currently lacks. Assume that no development land is available in the map grid squares B3 and C3. Suggest two different possible sites for each development.

Compare the possible access routes and the populations of some of the towns from which you might expect to attract visitors. Write two short reports explaining, in each case, which site would be more likely to bring income into the town.

1.9 The social impact of tourism in Calderdale

Develops knowledge and understanding of the following element:
1.4 Investigate the impact of the UK leisure and tourism industries

Supports development of the following core skills:
Application of number 3.3 (Task 1)
Application of number 3.1; Information Technology 3.1, 3.3 (Task 2)
Communication 3.2 (Task 3)

Tourism has been encouraged in Calderdale, mainly to try and counteract rising unemployment, and the fact that young people were leaving the area as traditional jobs were lost as mills closed. The influx of tourists brought some economic benefit to towns like Hebden Bridge, but assessment of the social impact of encouraging more visitors is more difficult to quantify.

Residents of the towns attracting the most visitors are affected in a number of ways, many of which may cause resentment. For example, local people may find that they have to:

- queue for longer in shops
- take more time to travel because of increased traffic
- face difficulty in locating parking spaces
- cope with overcrowded public transport
- share leisure facilities with visitors
- come to terms with rising property values.

A tourism impact study in Calderdale suggested that tourism had affected the provision of facilities which were also regarded as factors contributing to the quality of life of local residents. The table on page 22 summarises some of these impacts.

A major concern for residents of towns which see a rapid increase in the number of visitors is the question of loss of local identity. This is a particular worry where the popularity of the location leads outsiders to purchase second homes, either as holiday homes or in preparation for their retirement. The general effect of this is to push up house prices, and to

Facility	Tourism impact
Pubs	Become more crowded when tourist use is added to local use, but tourist trade may lead to extension of opening hours, so providing a benefit to local people too
Restaurants	May offer greater choice of food styles to cater for range of visitors, but making reservations becomes more difficult as popularity grows
Tea shops	Flourish in towns like Hebden Bridge, and others on popular tour routes, offering a service not previously available to local people at all
Churches	May find that tourism boosts their congregations and helps them to raise funds for restoration work, but local people may feel less a part of a very familiar group
Recreation facilities	Such as the ski centre in Calderdale, may depend on tourism for their financial viability, while the development of canal holidays and guided walks can be taken advantage of by both tourists and the local communities

put property out of reach of young and first-time buyers. The long-term effects of this are seen to be a raising of the average age of the local population, the moving away of young people from local communities and a general loss of community spirit. Though this view was expressed during surveys in Calderdale, some people also believed that tourism had increased their sense of identification with the area as a whole.

To some extent the social impact of tourism depends on how much contact there is between tourists and local residents. People's personal reactions to tourists may be hard to separate from their economic interests. For example, shopkeepers are likely to take a positive view because of the extra custom tourists bring; sheep farmers might feel more resentful because their contact with tourists is often over contentious issues such as rights of way, litter, failure to keep gates closed or harassment of animals by visitors' dogs.

It is not easy to measure the social impact of tourism. Most methods of testing this impact rely on the expressed opinions of local residents. For example, residents of Calderdale were asked what they thought were the positive and negative aspects of tourism in the region. The table below summarises their responses.

Benefits	Number of replies	%
None/don't know	50	20%
Economic	134	54%
Social/cultural	18	7%
Better promotion of the area	20	8%
Environmental	11	4%
More pressure on the Council	7	3%
More facilities	8	3%

Drawbacks	Number	%
None/don't know	104	42%
Increased traffic congestion	71	29%
Vandalism/pollution	16	6%
Higher prices	10	4%
Crowds	29	12%
Less originality	9	4%

Study the table below, showing how people in Calderdale thought tourism had affected them.

	Better (%)	Same (%)	Worse (%)	Don't know (%)
Employment	52	18	8	20
Income	45	27	9	19
Relaxation/entertainment	47	26	11	16
House prices	21	14	50	16
Condition of buildings	47	23	9	21
Traffic	5	8	76	12
Parking	5	8	73	15
Public transport	23	32	18	27
Access to countryside	32	36	12	20
State of countryside	19	33	29	18
Environmental quality	30	35	15	20
Shopping facilities	32	34	16	17
Community spirit	19	45	14	22
Own identity with Calderdale	17	49	11	22
Others	2	3	1	95

1 Identify which are regarded as the main positive and the main negative aspects of the social impact of tourism on Calderdale.

2 Select a local tourist destination and devise a questionnaire which will enable you to compare the social impact of tourism on Calderdale with its social impact on the destination you have selected.

3 Write a report outlining the similarities and differences of the social impact tourism has had on the two places. You should include an explanation of why you think the attitudes of the two resident communities are similar or different.

1.10 A new airport – the environmental impact

Develops knowledge and understanding of the following element:
1.4   Investigate the impact of the UK leisure and tourism industries

Supports development of the following core skills:
Communication 3.1, 3.4 (Task 1)
Communication 3.2 (Task 2)

Travel to many parts of the world has been revolutionised by the building of new airports. As facilities, airports tend to be measured in terms of the numbers of passengers who use them and, to a lesser extent, on the quality of the facilities available within them. It is less common to assess them in terms of their impact on the local environment and on the local people. Many of the larger modern airports evolved from small airfields and so were not originally planned with any notion of the volume of air traffic they now receive. In many cases their own growth stimulated an increase in the number of employees seeking homes in the vicinity, so that the surrounding areas are far more built up than could originally have been anticipated.

New airports have fewer excuses for not evaluating their likely environmental impact thoroughly. However, the economic prosperity of the country in which they are sited will influence the extent to which their designers build in features to protect the environment.

Noise is perhaps the most obvious example of an airport's impact. In many countries legislation will control the maximum noise levels permissible. Aircraft engine noise is particularly loud during take-off, initial climb and during the deceleration which takes place after landing. Longer runways could obviate the need for braking by using the noisy process of reversing the thrust of the engines. Aircraft engines are much quieter than they used to be but at times when the undercarriage and wheels are lowered turbulence increases the normal noise level. Some airports attempt to discourage older, louder types of jet aeroplane by charging them higher landing fees or requiring them to obtain special permission in order to land. All aircraft are divided into noise level categories which helps in monitoring the amount of noise at individual airports. Greater engine thrust means that modern jets can climb more steeply, thus reducing the noise at ground level after take-off.

One method of evaluating how much concern a larger airport has about noise is to measure the distance between the runways and the position and angle of take-off which they lead to in relation to the nearest settlements. Newer airports may have more space, which helps noise reduction, but they use up more land in achieving this. The airport authorities may also be judged on their voluntary efforts to reduce noise. They may impose restrictions on night flying. They may provide an extensive sound protection programme for local residents, installing double glazing and other forms of sound proofing. They may also carry out a regular noise monitoring procedure.

Air pollution has always been a concern in the vicinity of airports, with widespread beliefs that exhaust emissions and discharged fuel were a serious problem. Kerosene, used to fuel most aircraft, can be burned without much residue but some pollutants will still make their way into the atmosphere. It is not always easy, however, to establish where the main responsibility for air pollution lies, since road traffic, industry and private households

The siting of an airport has several implications for the environment.

may all disperse pollutants into the atmosphere in the vicinity of airports. Modern aircraft use less fuel than their predecessors, largely as a result of better design and reduced weight. Emergency landings can, however, require fuel to be dumped so that a safe landing weight can be achieved. This is usually done 5000 feet above the ground which means that the speed of the aircraft causes the fuel to disperse into tiny droplets which eventually evaporate.

The extent of air pollution in the vicinity of airports is, not surprisingly, governed by the amount of traffic. Pilots arriving at busier airports may find there is a queue waiting to land. Aeroplanes fly in holding patterns, circling the airport until there is a suitable landing opportunity. The rate of air pollution created at individual airports can be established by setting up monitoring stations to measure the concentration of pollutants such as sulphur dioxide, carbon monoxide, nitrogen oxides, hydrocarbons and dust.

The siting of a new airport has implications for the existing environment. The planners will wish to have approaches which are thinly populated, both to reduce the risk to the population and to limit the nuisance to them during and after construction. This usually means a countryside location with the accompanying problems of tree felling, drainage and wildlife disturbance. Larger airports will also demand the construction of a good transport network, as well as the means of supplying efficient power and sewage systems.

Airports are usually built on flat, low-lying land and this in turn usually means that there is some natural flow of groundwater present. Without care construction can interfere with this, lowering the water table and affecting land and wildlife in the surrounding areas. The foundations for airport runways need to be frost-proof and so the land used is drained so that the water cannot rise too close to the surface. Some newly constructed airports have systems of channelling water through dykes to reduce the impact on the surrounding water levels. Modern instruments can measure accurately both groundwater levels and chemical purity.

Measuring the quality of water in the surrounding areas is important since airports use a number of chemicals which harm the natural environment. In winter runways have to be kept free of ice and snow to make landings safe. Additionally the wings and fuselage of a departing aeroplane also have to have any ice removed. De-icing agents, using glycol, are employed. An airport sensitive to the environment will have installed systems preventing any contaminated meltwater being left in the ground. One modern method of doing this is to use bacteria to convert the glycol into water and carbon dioxide.

An airport generates a large amount of rubbish which can impose considerable strain on local refuse services. Though the local authority or private refuse collection company will have responsibility for removing the waste, the policy of the airport managers may indicate the level of their concern about the environment. For example, they may take responsibility for reducing its volume or recycling materials made of glass, paper or metal. Many of the airport operations which generate waste, such as catering, are likely to be franchised out to private companies so that some airport authorities might argue that the problem was often outside their control.

Runways, aircraft, airport buildings, perimeter fences and access roads cannot be said to improve the appearance of many environments. An airport can perhaps best be judged in this respect by the extent to which the developers have tried to limit the damage. Sometimes developers enter into an agreement to compensate for the loss of land use by creating landscape conservation areas around the perimeters. This can combine the creation of a nature reserve with an improvement in the visual appearance of the site. Its drawback is the cost and the fact that it may consume additional land. The use of low level buildings and the planting of trees and shrubs are indications that some consideration has been given to the airport's visual impact on the environment.

Some forms of wildlife, particularly larger birds which can be a risk to aircraft, are unwelcome at airports. Various visual and aural devices may be used to scare them off. Modern airports also plant vegetation such as forage grass which is not attractive either to larger birds or to ground insects which might attract feeding birds.

One aspect of an airport's impact on the environment which is often overlooked is their huge consumption of energy. Heating, lighting and refrigeration all require a power supply. Like all major energy users, the environmental impact can be reduced by economic working practices, such as installing good insulation and ensuring that heat and light systems are efficient enough not to provide excess.

Your tasks

1 Discuss the following questions arising from statements made in the text:

   a) On the basis of what facilities and services might a passenger assess the quality of an airport?

   What factors would be used by the local community to judge both the airport's impact and its performance ?

   b) Whose responsibility do you think it should be to assess the likely environmental impact of a new airport, particularly in an economically poor country?

   Who do you think should pay for any measures proposed to protect the environment around a new airport ?

   c) Identify the most common noises which annoy you. How many of these could be described as 'noise pollution'?

   Can you come up with a definition of 'noise pollution' which you think might enable legal action to be taken against anyone found to be contributing to it ?

   d) List the options available to an airport which decides that its monitoring stations are revealing an unacceptable level of air pollution.

   Which of these options do you think are practical courses of action and what consequences might they have, apart from attempting to reduce the air pollution?

   e) Suggest ways in which a farmer whose land abuts a new airport can judge its impact on his land and livestock.

   f) What reasons can you provide for supporting or opposing the view that it is possible to 'compensate' for the loss of wildlife habitat?`

2 Write a letter from a resident living in close proximity to an airport to whichever authority manages it.

   The content of the letter should assess what the resident believes has been the impact of the airport on him/herself and on the community in which they live.

Unit 2 Human resources in the leisure and tourism industries

2.1 Organisation and management at Beaulieu

Develops knowledge and understanding of the following element:
2.1   Investigate and compare organisational structures in leisure and tourism

Supports development of the following core skills:
Communication 3.1, 3.4 (Task 1)
Communication 3.4 (Task 2)
Communication 3.1 (Task 3)

Beaulieu is the name most visitors use for a number of attractions to be found on the Montagu family estate in Hampshire. The range of these attractions and the different activities and facilities available at each one means that the organisation is a very complex one.

Beaulieu employs monorail drivers, accountants, artists, photographers, teachers, gardeners, chefs, vehicle engineers, carpenters, archivists, receptionists, shop assistants, woodmen and even a harbour master! The work of all these individuals has to be co-ordinated so that the attraction as a whole benefits.

Most staff are part of a departmental structure, covering areas such as Projects and Services, Public Relations, Personnel, Accounts, Shops, Events, Information Centre, Motor Museum and Engineering, Special Features, Catering, and Education and Interpretation.

The whole organisation trades under the name of Montagu Ventures Limited and most income received is paid to this company. All the historic structures on the Montagu Estate are leased to the company and the costs of repairing and restoring them is met from visitor income. In addition the Beaulieu Estate benefits by receiving rents for the properties leased to Montagu Ventures.

Beaulieu employs a wide range of staff whose work needs to be well co-ordinated for the attraction to benefit.

At least one outside organisation is involved in the provision of services at Beaulieu. All the catering outlets are run, through a concession arrangement, by J. Lyons & Co. In return for allowing them to run catering outlets and charge customers, Lyons pay a proportion of the income they receive to Montagu Ventures.

The National Motor Museum is an independent charity. It receives income from donations and sponsorship, as well as receiving a proportion of the gate receipts. The National Motor Museum Trust, which manages the Museum, provides a team of specialist staff able to run library, research and educational services related to the history of motoring. They liaise closely with Montagu Ventures Ltd personnel who are responsible for all the services providing the public with access to the Museum.

Another working team, called Beaulieu River Management, organises the letting of berths and the arrangement of mooring fees. They too pay a proportion of this income to the Beaulieu Estate as rental for the facilities leased. The rural areas of the estate are managed by the Countryside Education Trust. This organisation is itself a registered charity with a separate Board of Trustees but it works very closely with Beaulieu's Education Department.

A centralised Accounts Department serves all these organisations except for the catering concessionaires. Each manager is dependent on the Accounts Department to produce up-to-date information to help them to run their part of the business efficiently. Records are used to provide regular analyses of profit or loss. The department also ensures that all money is paid into the bank, that all bills are settled, and that all wages and salaries are paid on time !

A management structure diagram is available to show who each department reports to and where they fit in the organisation as a whole. Managers are appointed because they have skills in specific areas, so the Retail Manager will have a background in retail and will understand the problems faced by the departmental team. The Catering Manager, an employee of J. Lyons, and the Curator, employed by the National Motor Museum Trust, are not employees of Montagu Ventures Ltd. It is important, however, that they are part of the management team to enable good communication between their own and other departments.

Most management structures are hierarchical, with a Managing Director at the top and a number of management levels below them. The number of levels at Beaulieu is small which keeps managers closer to their working teams and reduces the chances of an 'us and them' atmosphere among the work force. For individual projects teams of managers with special skills may be asked to work together on the development of new ideas.

Your tasks

Use the Montagu Ventures Management Structure diagram on the next page to answer the following questions.

I Discuss which manager listed on the diagram would be responsible for each of the following tasks:

   a) Drawing up plans for a future display interpreting the past history of the village of Beaulieu

   b) Meeting the manager of a London coach company thinking of including Beaulieu in a new coach tour

Montagu Ventures Management Structure

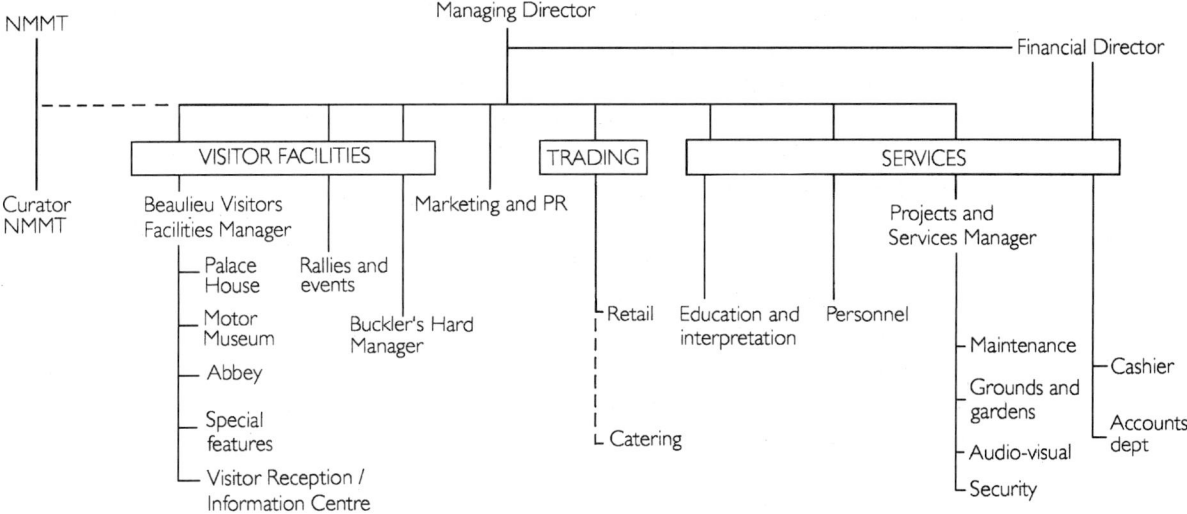

c) Reviewing the shops' stock control system

d) Administering the Classics and Restoration Show, a one-day rally at Beaulieu for specialist car clubs

e) Delivering a training session on the subject of uniform and appearance to new staff.

2 Suggest suitable management teams for the development of the following new projects:

a) A summer season cruise from Buckler's Hard, on the Beaulieu estate, with an on-board evening meal and a live music performance included

b) The replacement of all the existing outdoor signage at Beaulieu and Buckler's Hard with newly designed signs

c) A charity event in which, for an agreed donation, participants accompany a celebrity in a veteran car drive from Beaulieu to Brighton

d) A *son-et-lumiere* show planned to illustrate almost 800 years in the history of Beaulieu Abbey

e) A mail order service offering video films featuring various aspects of motoring and motor racing history.

3 Discuss, in each case, which manager would be the most appropriate person to take overall long term responsibility for each of these projects if it was decided to approve and implement them.

2.2 Teamwork and motivation

Develops knowledge and understanding of the following element:
2.2 Investigate how leisure and tourism teams operate

Supports development of the following core skills:
Communication 3.1 (Task 1)
Application of number 3.2, 3.3 (Task 2)

An outsider's view of a successful company will often focus on individuals within it who carry the highest profile, perhaps the Chairman or the Managing Director. However the success is almost certainly dependent on good teamwork since there are very few companies where the managers do not spend a significant part of their time working with departmental or project groups.

To work effectively in a team people have to believe in the value and benefit of working in this way. It requires the company to create a sense that being part of a team increases rather than decreases the importance of individuals. The atmosphere has to be right too. For people to work successfully with others, there has to be trust and a respect for the skills and abilities of other people. Jealousy, negative criticism, and personal competitiveness need to be reduced if the team is to function well.

Not all teams, even if they accept the company ethos and philosophy, will behave in the same way. The nature of the tasks they are given, and the time and resources allowed, may affect their working relationships. If they have been told to do something they may react differently from the way they would respond if they had been consulted or taken part in the decision-making process. They are more likely to be positive if the group has clearly defined objectives, a known means of communicating its views and a belief that its recommendations will be acted on.

The combination of individuals in a team requires thought. Strong characters may clash; the more reticent may prove indecisive. The dynamics of the group may change as they get to know each other better, either gaining confidence in what they are doing or losing enthusiasm when problems are encountered. Even when a team is working together, it is important that the particular skills of individuals are identified and used to their full potential. For example, there is not much to be gained by rotating the responsibility for writing minutes of team meetings if two members of the team, who may be good at other things, prove quite unable to do it competently. Some individuals may be good planners; some may be good conversationalists, able to put others quickly at ease; some may be very practical in terms of converting ideas into working products and systems.

There are a number of factors which are essential for good teamwork. The size of the group should be appropriate to the task. A committee required to come up with a health and safety report in a small business might find it hard to produce clear conclusions if 20 people were on it. A full investigation into a major aircraft failure might fail to gather sufficient evidence if it depended on a team of two. The team needs clear objectives and a recognised means of making its conclusions known in the right quarters. The team can be helped to feel a sense of achievement if its work results in action or change. It may be that having a limited time frame will help to sustain momentum and keep the approaches of individuals to the task fresh.

Providing a team with its own working space is also important in motivating them. It shows what value is put on the work they are doing and increases their sense of identification with the task or project. Motivating the team is, however, likely to be more dependent on other factors such as the perceived importance of the work being done by the team. The level of interest shown by managers in individual tasks will indicate this. Sharing decisions and learning new skills and knowledge can also be important motivating factors. Sensitively handled, appraisal systems can be a valuable means of recognising individual contributions to a team and to a company as a whole.

Your tasks

1 The travel agency, Better Getaway Holidays, employs four regional sales teams based in Manchester (for the North), in Birmingham (for the Midlands), Bristol (for the West), and London (for the South).

After a moderate year, the company wishes to increase its sales. Discuss which of the following methods you think would be most likely to motivate the regional sales teams most to improve their sales figures:

a) Offer a free weekend holiday in Paris for the team making the most sales over a 6-month period

b) Send each team a report of the sales performance of all the regional teams and ask them to account for the differences

c) Provide a week's fresh training for all teams together in a Bournemouth hotel

d) Offer the possibility of promotion to run new sales teams for Wales and Scotland to those with the best sales performance over a 6-month period

e) Suggest that redundancies will be necessary if sales do not improve

f) Stage a two-day conference for all sales teams to plan a strategy for improving future sales performance

g) Arrange for the Managing Director to visit each team individually, to express appreciation for their past efforts, and to outline hopes for the company's future

h) Offer a cash bonus to individual sales staff of £5 for every holiday sold.

2 Consider the sales figures for Better Getaway Holidays for 1991 and 1992 as shown in the table below.

Draw up a plan of action which would enable the company to use these figures to motivate rather than discourage the members of the four regional sales teams.

Better Getaway Holidays annual sales figures

	1990			1991		
	Number of holiday packages	Average value	Total sales	Number of holiday packages	Average value	Total sales
North Region	2000	300	600 000	2100	325	682 500
Midlands Region	1500	350	525 000	1600	325	520 000
West Region	1200	350	420 000	1400	350	490 000
South Region	3000	350	1 050 000	2000	350	700 000
Total	7700	337.50	2 595 000	7100	337.50	2 392 500

2.3 Leadership

Develops knowledge and understanding of the following element:
2.2   Investigate how leisure and tourism teams operate

Supports development of the following core skills:
Communication 3.1 (Task 1)
Communication 3.2, 3.3 (Task 2)
Communication 3.1 (Task 3)

It is rare in any team exercise for each individual participant to make an identical contribution. Some are inevitably more influential than others. They may actually try to bully or dominate others. This may make them appear to be strong characters but does not make them good leaders since they are likely to overlook the potential of other group members.

The popular concept of leadership is often linked with famous figures from the past such as Churchill, Kennedy or Martin Luther King. These figures are generally remembered for their eloquence and forceful personalities. Yet there are many ways of getting people to do things apart from rhetoric and personal charisma. Leaders should aim to get people to do things because they want to, not because they are afraid or blinded by hero worship. Eisenhower described leadership as 'the art of getting someone else to do something you want done because he wants to do it'.

Any working team needs common goals. Each person in the team is likely to have different potential, in terms of their character and in terms of their skills and interests. They may all have some leadership qualities, such as being a good listener, having the ability to plan ahead, or communicating effectively with others. The art of leadership is that whoever assumes that role, whether permanently or just for a specific part of the task, is able to make the maximum use of the collective potential available. Simply dictating terms to the rest of the team is wasteful and is likely in the long run to demoralise the group.

There are many practical reasons why leaders should share responsibilities. People are more likely to complete tasks efficiently and with enthusiasm if they feel their ideas have been a valued factor in the process. They feel a sense of ownership of the task. Some tasks are in any case too time-consuming to be completed by leaders or managers and so they must depend on others. They have to delegate tasks and responsibilities appropriately, so that members of a team feel that they know what they are doing and that the responsibility given measures up to their experience and skills.

Leaders must be able to pass on their commitment to the task or organisation since, otherwise, perfectly able team members may refuse to recognise the importance or purpose of a particular project. The relationship between leaders and followers can be affected by a range of personal factors. Trust is essential and can only be gained if the leader acts with integrity towards others and is seen to set a good example. Depending on the team and the task this may require vision, tact, sympathy, encouragement, detailed planning, expert knowledge, good communication, an ability to demonstrate, a willingness to share the burden of work, or any combination of these.

Some people see leadership as simply exercising control. An example of this style has been light-heartedly characterised as the 'seagull style of management', where the boss is constantly hovering over people's shoulders and, when things go wrong, immediately

Effective leadership means managers and staff looking together for ways to meet company objectives.

drops the responsibility on them. However most recent studies of leadership have suggested that vision is the most important factor in achieving success. This involves identifying needs, developing ideas which can achieve them, communicating these to working teams, and sustaining a high level of motivation in the work force. It is a style which requires leaders to set an example to others, to encourage others to be active, and to look together for ways of improving what they do and how they do it. This obviously implies that if team members or employers are unable to meet their objectives, leaders will not be able to achieve theirs either.

The individual members of any team have different personalities. Effective leaders need to be able to make contact with individuals and gain their respect. They can't do this if they give instructions and then disappear! Personal contact shows they are interested and ensures they understand better all stages of the working process, as well as making individuals feel more important. Improving self-confidence and self-esteem within a team quickly raises morale and motivation. Insisting that team members know their place and do not compete for the limelight with managers often has the opposite effect. If a task is to be successfully completed, it should be done the best way. Good leaders do not insist that their way of doing things is always the only acceptable method of getting the job done.

There are other reasons for encouraging the development of leadership qualities. Most teams will require new leaders at some point in the future and it is important to identify those who will fulfil the role most effectively. Many individuals need an image of their future potential development. It helps to guide their ideas about what they are doing and to develop their individual strengths. It is not easy to motivate someone who feels that their role will remain unchanged indefinitely.

To sum up, good leadership is about changing attitudes and methods so that tasks can be completed in what all those working on them agree is the best way.

Your tasks

1 Divide into groups of four or five. Consider each of the following tasks in turn:

a) Planning and publishing the schedule of activities for a newly-opened sports hall

b) Organising a 'Tidy Up Our Village' campaign

c) Designing and making an award for the restaurant in your region judged to offer the best welcome to customers

d) Planning a sponsored event to raise funds for enhancing the leisure activities available in a local community centre

e) Establishing a nature trail suitable for 8–13-year-olds.

Discuss the roles and responsibilities you think members of the group would have to take on in order to complete each of these tasks.

Consider what kind of leadership you think would be appropriate for a team intending to tackle each task.

List the qualities needed and then appoint each member of the group as project leader for one of the above tasks.

2 Each member of the group should prepare an initial briefing for the others about the nature of the task they have agreed to lead and how they propose the group should approach it. They should then make a short presentation developing their ideas.

3 Each presentation should then be evaluated in terms of the leadership qualities which the group had earlier identified as being important to each specific task.

2.4 Conflict and co-operation at work

Develops knowledge and understanding of the following element:
2.2 Investigate how leisure and tourism teams operate

Supports development of the following core skills:
Communication 3.1 (Task 1)
Communication 3.1 (Task 2)

Most people are fortunate enough to have friends. They may be people with shared interests, with similar personalities, of similar age, or with any combination of these factors. Though they may disagree about individual issues, they each find likeable characteristics in the other. Working teams may contain friends, but it is equally likely that they will contain individuals who are either indifferent to each other or, worse, experience a mutual dislike.

Animosity or aggression is rarely constructive in a work situation. Personal dislikes can easily lead to criticism and mistrust, both of which will contribute to an atmosphere in which people find it difficult to work effectively. However, many personal dislikes are too strong to change. It is the task of the manager or team leader to establish trust and respect for each individual. This may be done through raising awareness of the rights and responsibilities of everyone involved in the work team.

The easiest atmosphere in which to work with someone you do not like is one where the importance of achieving overall objectives is agreed and where standards of judging

Staff serving in a restaurant may pass on pressure to serve quickly onto staff working in the kitchens.

individual contributions are consistently applied. Everybody should be accountable for what they do and there should be no evident favouritism, especially where rewards or concessions are concerned.

A number of factors may give rise to conflict within work teams. The pressures of the job may be the most common one, for example where staff waiting at table in a busy restaurant are passing the pressure to be served quickly which they receive from customers onto staff working in the kitchens. All of us are subject to changes of mood. The consequences of a domestic row or a difficult journey to work can lead some personalities into conflict with the next human target – their colleagues at work. Some companies send managers and employees on training courses aimed at raised their levels of self-awareness and awareness of others in the belief that such training can reduce conflict.

Poor communication is a common cause of conflict at work. Tasks which are not explained clearly, messages which are indecipherable or not passed on at all, and documentation which is inaccurate create resentment, usually targeted at an individual perpetrator. The manner of spoken communication can also cause resentment, particularly if junior employees feel they are being patronised or criticised unreasonably.

Whatever precautions are taken, most companies will experience lack of co-operation from individuals or work teams from time to time. A team of waiters may feel that one of their number is too slow and is leaving them with more work to do. A museum guide may make it evident to visitors that they are less than enthusiastic about the collection. To solve these conflicts and ensure future co-operation someone has to confront them. The first task here is to identify accurately both who is responsible and the likely causes of conflict.

The task of resolving conflict usually lies with managers. If they decree solutions without consultation they are unlikely to remove the resentment. If they lose the respect and sympathy of those responsible it may be difficult to win them back in the future. In industries like leisure and tourism, which are so dependent on people, the answer to most conflicts and disputes should be personal. As a recent article addressed to leisure managers suggested, 'people's performance does nothing more nor less than reflect your expectation and the way that they are treated.'

Your tasks

1 **a)** List what you consider to be your own strengths and weaknesses.

   b) List six of your own general likes and dislikes about other people's behaviour.

   c) Discuss whether any of these could lead to conflict in a work situation and what the best way of resolving such conflict would be.

2 Your school/college has a small but valuable collection of paintings or manuscripts and decides to open these to public view. Personnel to implement this are to be drawn from your own student group.

   Three of the functions you will need to provide are teams of between 3 and 5 people to:
   ● design a brochure advertising the collection
   ● act as guides for visitors
   ● plan the financial management of the scheme.

   Discuss which individuals would make the best combinations for each of these three teams and why. Unless there are fewer than 9 of you, no person should appear in more than one team.

2.5 Games as teamwork training

Develops knowledge and understanding of the following element:
2.2 Investigate how leisure and tourism teams operate

Supports development of the following core skills:
Communication 3.1 (Task 1)
Communication 3.1 (Task 2)
Communication 3.1 (Task 3)
Communication 3.1 (Task 4)
Communication 3.1 (Task 5)

Learning to work with others is generally a gradual process. Many companies feel it involves skills which can be encouraged by a variety of training methods, including role plays, simulations and games. These activities have the advantage over training in a real work context in that they are controlled and short term. This means performances can be quickly analysed and key skills identified without interrupting normal daily work processes. The activities can be structured to focus on specific skills or qualities. They can require participants to adopt other roles than their usual working ones, making them more adaptable and more aware of the perceptions of others who work with them.

A typical training session aimed at building up teamwork skills might begin with an 'ice breaker' – a game intended to get participants talking to each other. An example might be that partners have to describe the best holiday they ever had to each other and then report back their partner's experience to the whole group. Stickers might be placed on the back of each participant, one set giving a range of dates, the other giving corresponding famous events which happened on those days. Finding the partner with the corresponding label establishes verbal contact in a context which is fun.

Communication is an essential part of good teamwork and there are many games designed to improve this. Most focus on the spoken word, perhaps largely because the majority of day-to-day work communication is likely to be oral. A common example is the game where one person has a note pad or flip chart and faces away from their partner. The partner is given a drawing or diagram and has to give instructions so that it can be drawn with reasonable accuracy. Two-way communication can be encouraged by allowing the 'artist' to ask questions. Pressure to work together more effectively can be introduced by the setting of a time limit, or by restricting answers to questions to 'yes' or 'no'.

Sometimes the purpose of the training may be as much about the way things are said as about what is said. Role plays, simulating real work situations, can meet this need, particularly with reasonably experienced employees. Some trainers will film or record these performances and then analyse them. While this may be appropriate for those with the confidence or seniority to handle it, it is likely to inhibit many people. Games where participants have to say given sentences or phrases in different ways, sometimes regardless of their meaning, are a gentler introduction. They can be asked to emphasise underlined words, or speak them with different feelings – sympathy, irritation, or amusement for example.

Setting a puzzle is a common method of getting a team to begin to work co-operatively. This can be a relatively simple exercise, such as assembling a number of irregular shapes so that they form a recognisable geometric figure or arranging a random series of words into the longest comprehensible sentence possible. An element of competition can both increase the fun and stimulate individuals to build on the ideas of others. A game which requires both co-operation and communication is called the Newspaper Race. Teams are given identical piles of randomly mixed newspaper sheets, each pile made up from the complete contents of five different newspapers. Each team sits in a line, in single file so that they can only see the back of the person in front. The object of the game is for each team to reassemble the original five newspapers. Clearly good communication and organisation are essential!

Many teamwork games encourage the development of roles within the group. This would apply to the games which include an element of designing or building. A popular example requires each team to design and make a full set of clothing for one individual using only newspaper and Sellotape. If all five members of a team work on design at the same time, or if they all watch one person sticking together a jacket, the value of being in a team may be shown up by the efforts of a group which plans its efforts jointly. Design and make exercises are a useful means of seeing whether different skills can be harnessed by a team. One individual may be very creative, another very dextrous, and a third good at planning an effective schedule.

Another category is the kind of game intended to build up the level of trust between working colleagues. Outward bound courses usually contain a strong element of this, encouraging a sense of physical reliance on both the individual and the team as a whole. On a simpler level is the game which requires members of a team to line up in two rows facing each other. Starting quite close to one another, a fresh egg is thrown in such a way that it can be caught by the person opposite without it breaking. The thrower retires to the back of the team and hence the distance thrown gradually increases. The team establishing the longest distance between thrower and successful catcher wins. Needless to say, best working clothes are rarely worn for this game!

Some games are intended to increase the sense of shared purpose in a team. Especially in leisure and tourism, the way customers perceive individual companies or attractions is

Many companies use training to develop good team-work among their staff.

affected by the attitude of the staff. Games aimed at developing a sense of company ethos may include writing acrostics based on the name of the company or attraction or on some words crucial to its success, such as *visitors*, *image* or *presentation*. Discussion of the ideas composed by the participants draws attention to the company's philosophy and what it hopes all its staff are striving for.

Your tasks

Working in different teams for each activity, take part in each of the following games, some of which will require some prior planning:

1 An ice breaker
Each participant receives a sticker, placed unseen on his or her back, on which the name of a city is written. The object of the game is for all participants to arrange themselves so that the names of the towns read in alphabetical order.

2 Did you hear the news today?
Select teams of 4 or 5 people. One member of each team goes out of the room and listens to a prerecorded news item or reads a magazine feature article. Making sure that they cannot be overheard, they describe its contents to a second member of the team, who in turn passes it on to a third, and so on until it reaches the last member of the team. The accounts given by each final team member are compared and the factors accounting for the differences discussed.

3 It's the way you tell them!
Study a paragraph from a school or college text book until you are very familiar with its content. Take it in turns to read it out as if you were:

- handing out a reprimand at work
- reading a love story
- commentating on the final three furlongs of the Grand National
- doing the voice-over for a TV perfume commercial
- practising your DJ patter
- selling a second hand car
- soothing an irate customer
- taking part in a family argument.

4 Solve this

Draw this diagram on a flip chart.

Each team should attempt to agree on how many squares they can see. They should nominate a team member to explain their answer to the other teams.

5 Trust me

Each team represents the news gathering team of a different and rival tabloid newspaper, each of which is keen to discredit the others. Unknown to the other groups, each team agrees that one of its members has a secret – entirely fictional but one they would wish to keep confidential. Each team member pairs off with a team member from another team in an attempt to gather a good story for his or her own newspaper. At the end of an agreed time the newspaper groups re-form and draft their planned front page stories. These are then compared to see to what extent confidentiality has been honoured.

2.6 Teamwork and presenting a good case

Develops knowledge and understanding of the following element:

2.2 Investigate how leisure and tourism teams operate

Supports development of the following core skills:

Communication 3.1, 3.2 (Task 1)
Communication 3.1 (Task 2)

Easthampton Museum has been in existence since 1878. The Padgett family began the collection by donating paintings and items gathered by Lord Padgett during his travels. A combination of further bequests and sensible purchasing policies by the Museum's Management Trust meant that, for a provincial museum, the collection was considered interesting enough by the 1950s to compare favourably with those in a number of much larger cities. Thereafter the level of funding gradually declined, however, so much so that currently the Museum finds itself in some financial difficulty.

Four groups have a particular interest in the Museum's future. They are:

- **The Museum Management Committee**: this small team is aware that the Museum is in urgent need of modernisation, both because some areas are looking increasingly dilapidated and because few young people are attracted. They have a strong desire to preserve the Museum's existing function as a place to exhibit artistic and cultural items. They are aware of the need to increase revenue if the Museum is to survive

- **The Friends of the Museum**: this small society has elected a committee to see that their interests are represented. The group contains people with a passion for art and history, including both leisure and academic interests. They are very concerned about what they feel is the steady erosion of local leisure services

- **Kind Arts plc**: aware of the Museum's financial difficulties, this company is preparing to submit a plan to convert the Museum into a mixed arts centre which will reduce the exhibition space and replace some of it with a cinema, a small theatre and an underground bowling alley. They have appointed a small project team to ensure that their scheme is considered alongside any other proposals for the Museum's future

- **Easthampton Borough Council**: the small team in the Leisure and Recreation Department is aware of recent public criticism of local leisure facilities. They have no funds available for any major development work, but they are seeking ways of raising the profile of the town in the hope of attracting more outside visitors. However the Council itself reveals a considerable division of opinion about the kind of image the town should seek to develop. Some are strongly for maintaining its traditional historical associations; others argue that it is failing to keep pace with the modern world.

The museum's three best known exhibits have, not surprisingly, been the focus of much recent speculation. A brief description follows of each one.

The Kumbet Vases: brought from Turkey in 1816 by Sir George Devonshire. Two matching marble vases depicting figures. The Turkish government claims they are part of their heritage and should be returned. A New York private collector has offered £3 million for them.

Nightmare: a painting by the abstract American artist, Elmer Lewis, donated in 1970 by Lady Padgett. A 15-foot square black canvas half-covered in red hand prints. The painting was described by one critic as resembling 'the product of a huge, unimaginative class of primary school children'. A major art dealer has valued it at £250 000.

The Kratzburg Fragment: an Anglo-Saxon manuscript, part of a much longer account of eighth-century life in North Germany. In a very fragile condition and no longer easy to read. However, because it is a unique record, regarded as priceless.

A discussion on local television, watched by representatives of each of the four groups already mentioned, raises six possible courses of action, though arguments are raised for and against each of them.

Each of the six proposals is followed by some of the comments made about them:

1 'We should offer to sell one of the vases to New York for £1.5 million and return the other to the Turkish government.'
   a) '. . .the vases were made as a pair and should always be exhibited as a pair. Separating them would be artistic vandalism. . .'
   b) '. . .neither New York nor Turkey would be satisfied by this offer...'
   c) '. . .the Turks would regard it as an insult to be offered half of what they regard as theirs in the first place. . .'
   d) '. . .selling to a New York private collector would mean that the general public would no longer be able to admire one of the vases. . .'

2 'We should charge visitors an extra entrance fee of £2 to view a new modern art section, which would include *Nightmare'*.
   a) '. . .museums should be for everyone, not just for those who can afford to pay. . .'
   b) '. . .we should try to educate visitors to appreciate modern art, and not set it apart as if it were something different and difficult to understand. . .'
   c) '. . .visitors would complain that they were being exploited. . .'

3 'We should advertise The Kratzburg Fragment for sale in American art collecting magazines for a price to be negotiated.'
   a) '. . .it is a valuable piece of European history, and does not belong in America. . .'
   b) '. . .it could pass into the hands of someone who does not know how to conserve it successfully. . .'
   c) '. . .we could gain the reputation of being more interested in profit than in having unique artefacts in our collection. . .'
   d) '. . .there's not much point in renovating the building if there's nothing of outstanding interest on display inside it. . .'

4 'We should offer to sell The Kumbet Vases to the Turkish government for £3 million.'
   a) '. . .the Turkish people are not wealthy enough to meet that asking price. . .'
   b) '. . .the vases rightfully belong to Turkey, having been sold previously by rulers who ignored the importance of heritage to their people. . .'
   c) '. . .putting them up for auction could successfully raise a higher bid than £3 million. . .'

5 'We should offer to exchange the *Nightmare* painting for a more traditional picture, for example an oil painting of an English landscape.'
   a) '. . .I can't think of anyone who would be willing to make such an exchange. . .'
   b) '. . .we already have oil paintings of English landscapes in our collection. . .'
   c) '. . .it is our responsibility as a museum to cater for a variety of interests, including minority tastes. . .'

6 'We should remove The Kratzberg Fragment to the safety of a vault away from public view, where it can be more effectively preserved.'
   a) '. . .there is no point in keeping it if no-one is going to see it. . .'

b) '. . .we can't afford to have such a valuable asset serving no active purpose in the museum. . .'

c) '. . .though preservation techniques may extend its life, it can't last for ever. . .'

Your tasks

1 Divide into 4 teams, representing:
   - The Museum Management Committee
   - The Friends of Easthampton Museum
   - Kind Arts plc (project team)
   - Easthampton Borough Council (leisure and recreation)

   Discuss your reactions to the proposals and comments which resulted from the television programme.

   Reach an agreement about which single proposal your group would give its full support to and prepare a short press release expressing your views.

2 Each group should now meet with each of the other groups in turn and attempt to establish the following:
   - their main areas of agreement
   - their main areas of disagreement
   - issues over which they think a compromise might be reached.

2.7 Career opportunities

Develops knowledge and understanding of the following element:
2.3 Investigate, and prepare for, recruitment and selection in leisure and tourism

Supports development of the following core skills:
Communication 3.2, 3.4 (Task 1)
Communication 3.2 (Task 2)

Leisure and tourism is an industry which attracts a range of new entrants, including school leavers and graduates. At one time it had the reputation of offering only seasonal unskilled or semi-skilled employment, but it now clearly offers a broad range of skilled, supervisory and management roles.

Your tasks

1 Use the information provided in the flow chart on page 10 to prepare a short talk about the career opportunities available in hotel work.

2 List the personal qualities which might be thought appropriate for hotel work at semi-skilled, skilled, supervisory or management levels.

3 Choose a working environment in Leisure and Tourism, other than a hotel, which offers a range of career opportunities. You might select from the following:
- heritage centre
- tour operator
- major theme park
- transport company
- museum
- arts complex.

Create a flow chart showing possible entry points into this area of work, the qualifications required at different levels, and the possible career development.

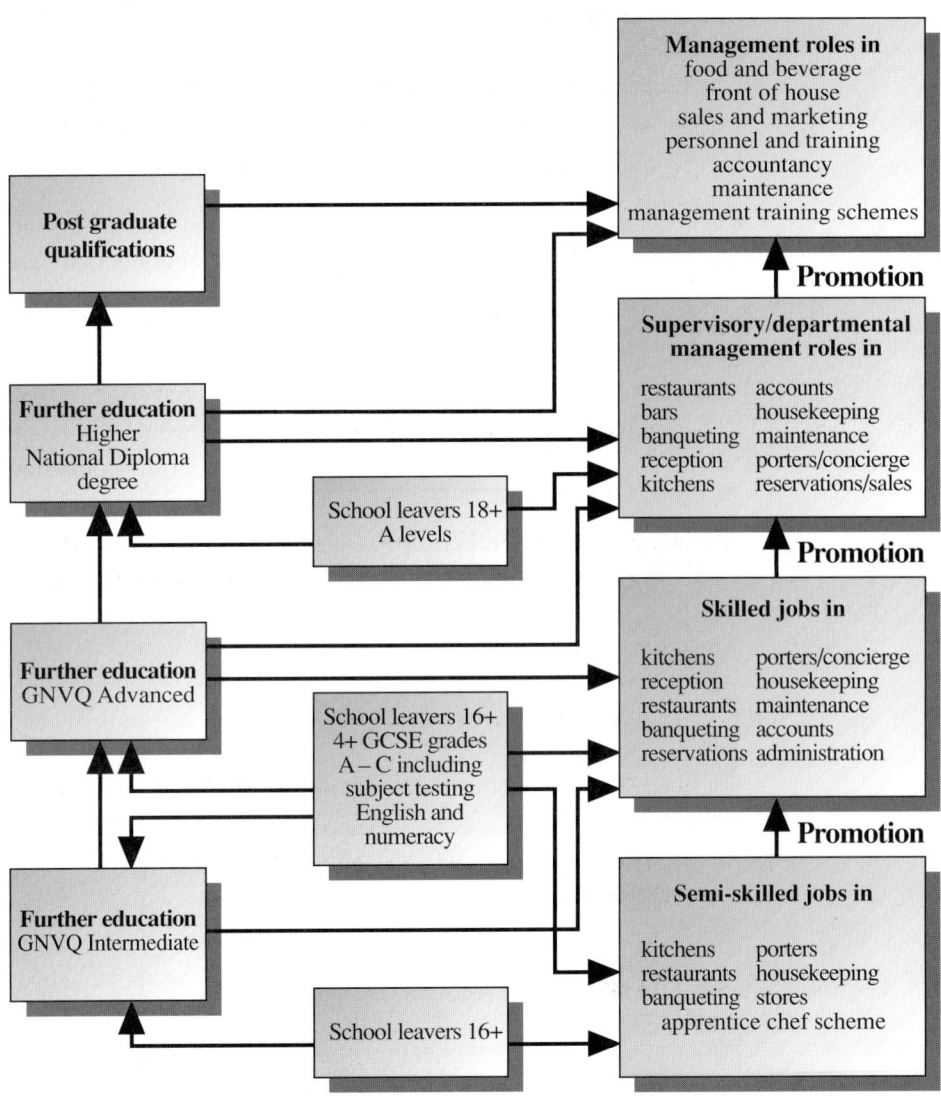

Opportunities flow chart. An example of possible entry points into hotel work.

2.8 Recruitment and selection procedures: Thomas Cook Retail Travel

Develops knowledge and understanding of the following element:

2.3 Investigate, and prepare for, recruitment and selection in leisure and tourism

Supports development of the following core skills:
Communication 3.2, 3.4 (Task 1)
Communication 3.2, 3.4 (Task 2)
Communication 3.1, 3.2; Information Technology 3.1, 3.3 (Task 3)
Communication 3.1 (Task 4)
Communication 3.1 (Task 5)
Communication 3.1 (Task 6)
Communication 3.1 (Task 7)
Communication 3.1 (Task 8)

When vacancies become available in a retail travel business, larger companies are most likely to consider first whether there are any suitable internal candidates. These people would already have an understanding of the ethos and operating practices of the company, and would therefore cost less to train. Additionally, it is important to provide opportunities for promotion or career changes of direction to existing staff. This makes them feel more valued and keeps morale high.

An individual branch of a travel agency chain would, in the absence of any suitable internal candidates, be likely to use an advertising agency. This agency would agree the design of the advertisement with the retail company and ensure that it was placed in appropriate local and trade newspapers. The positioning of the advertisement is very important. The agency would aim to have it placed in a prominent position on the page, preferably ensuring that it was not on the same page as advertisements of the company's main competitors. For example, Thomas Cook and Lunn Poly, both of whose logos are red, would not expect to have advertisements for new staff placed next to each other. Thomas

Sales Consultant
TRAVEL

Location   Salary

If you have plenty of initiative and are keen to develop a career in travel, why not do so with one of the most reputable names in the business. Thomas Cook.

We can develop your skills with thorough training, we can help you work towards professional qualifications, and we can encourage you to acquire an all-round knowledge of our varied business which goes way beyond booking holidays.

First, you must have experience in a sales and/or customer service role which has proved your ability to help customers, build a rapport and work well in a team.

If you can provide quality service - and achieve sales - in a fast-changing environment the career prospects are excellent. So too are the initial rewards: a competitive salary and benefits such as profit share and an incentive scheme which gives generous discounts on holidays.

Thomas Cook
Travel

For an application form please phone (number) between 9am and 5.30pm Monday to Friday.

Closing date for completed applications:

Sample Thomas Cook advertisement for a sales consultant.

Cook, the parent company, produces a manual for branch managers which contains a number of sample layouts with standard text for a number of different job vacancies. These will all stress some common issues, such as the emphasis on teamwork, the importance of customer service, the need for an outgoing personality and the need for an ability to work effectively under pressure. Each of these sample advertisements is then tailored to meet the specific requirements of the job advertised.

Once a job has been advertised and responses received, a process of short-listing takes place. The short-listing is usually based on a number of criteria. These criteria are applied to the letters, application forms and curriculum vitae (CVs) of applicants. In retail travel a personnel manager would probably use all or some of the following criteria in deciding which candidates were worthy of calling for interview:

1 evidence of customer service skills
2 evidence of sales ability
3 evidence of adaptability, e.g. learning new skills, time management, responding to different types of customer
4 ability to cope under pressure
5 experience of and attitude to working in teams
6 evidence of an ability to communicate effectively
7 evidence of the work standards they set for themselves.

Candidates for most jobs are asked to provide the names of referees. Referees are asked to give their view about the candidate's suitability for the job for which they have applied. In retail travel, references are generally not taken up until the job is actually offered to a candidate. This ensures confidentiality for job applicants who may not wish their current employers to know that they are applying for jobs elsewhere. However, the job offer is always made subject to the references provided being satisfactory. The offer may be withdrawn if the references show that the candidate had performed poorly at work, or if they had had unacceptable levels of absence, or if they had been the subject of disciplinary action.

The interview is regarded as the critical part of the selection process. However, the format of interviews is likely to vary according to the type of job being advertised. The traditional question and answer approach may be supplemented by written tests or role plays. Thomas Cook, for example, generally involves two interviewers in the process – one to ask questions and the other to note responses. Notes taken during the interview help to determine afterwards how successfully the candidate has measured up to the company's expectations. Some companies, such as Forte Hotels, use a screening assessment form during interviews. This enables interviewers to award ratings on a points scale against criteria like:

- personal image and appearance
- previous experience
- health record
- leadership qualities
- enthusiasm
- response to pressure
- initiative
- attention to detail
- communication skills
- commercial awareness.

Successful candidates usually receive confirmation of a job offer in writing. Thomas Cook send a copy of their conditions of employment with this offer letter, and this must be signed and returned to indicate formal acceptance of the job. Unsuccessful candidates generally have to ask if they want some feedback about how they performed in the interview and why they were not successful. In retail travel the common reasons for unsuccessful job applications are unacceptable standards of customer service and a failure to establish a good rapport with other people, essential qualities in such a people-focused industry.

The law requires the job selection process to be non-discriminatory. In other words race or gender must not be used as grounds for judging any candidate's suitability. Thomas Cook's advertising agency fills in a response analysis sheet for all advertisements placed. This produces data about those who reply to the advertisement, and categorises them according to gender, race and how able bodied they are. In Northern Ireland, the religions of respondents are also checked. If analysis of these data reveals any clear imbalance in the types of response, the company will review the pattern of where its advertisements are placed to try and encourage a more representative response in future.

Example of a person and role profile for a travel sales consultant

Factor	Profile of ideal person
Knowledge and experience	– sound knowledge of the products sold – good knowledge of travel geography – relevant qualifications, e.g. BA Fares & Ticketing – experience of cash handling and acceptable payment methods – ability to arrange complex itineraries – good knowledge of company practice and regulations – sound knowledge of accountancy documentation, sources of reference and security procedures
Human relations skills	– ability to communicate effectively face to face, by phone and in writing – ability to establish good rapport with customers – tenacity in closing a sale – ability to work as a member of a team
Thinking and reasoning	– ability to match customer needs to most appropriate company product – ability to balance consideration for company profit and cost with maintenance of quality service – ability to identify additional opportunities for sales and revenue generation, e.g. foreign exchange
Numerical, logical and information technology skills	– ability to use appropriate Computer Reservations Systems – knowledge of manual and automated ticketing – ability to perform arithmetic calculations accurately and quickly – ability to understand complex booking quotes
Personal qualities	– ability to operate under pressure and cope with customer peaks – patience and calmness in dealing with customers – willingness to take decisions and work unsupervised within agreed responsibilities – pride in appearance and presentation – friendly, enthusiastic and outgoing personality
Physical skills	– dexterity in using a keyboard, paperwork and cash – ability to cope with long periods sitting at a desk – ability to use video display unit (VDU) for prolonged periods – quick reaction to frame requests

An important part of the recruitment and selection process is the creation of job descriptions and person specifications. Job descriptions provide a clear statement to applicants about what they will be expected to do. A job description will outline the role the successful candidate will fill. Some companies set out job descriptions in the form of a list of responsibilities and duties. Thomas Cook prefer to describe the skills required and the performance standards expected from an employee fulfilling a specific role. They will include reference to the type of tasks required, but will also include targets such as sales performance. The job description may form the basis of a person specification. This is more for the benefit of the company seeking to recruit, as it clarifies the particular qualities and experience they think are appropriate for the specific job being advertised.

Most jobs in travel require candidates to complete application forms and to submit a CV. The application forms will often require candidates to identify aspects of their own experience which have enabled them to develop personal qualities and work-related skills. The increasing use of word processors and consultants giving professional advice about CVs means that presentation appears to be becoming more standardised. It is therefore very important that a CV makes direct reference to the requirements of the specific job being advertised. A good CV should make the recruiter feel that its author is particularly interested in the job and is not routinely applying for anything which comes along. Length is not often regarded as praiseworthy in a CV. People may not have time to read detailed descriptions of applicants' full career histories. They are more likely to take note of the key career moves, the main achievements and the training record of the applicant. Generally speaking, most recent experience will carry more weight than things done a long time ago. However, in any summary of a career history, it is advisable to provide an explanation of any gaps in employment.

Interviews often decide whether or not a candidate is selected for a job. There is no end of advice about how to approach interviews. A personnel manager for a major retail travel chain suggested these pointers to success:

- try to make a good first impression, both through your appearance and through trying to find out something about the company to whom you're applying
- be as honest and open as you can, and admit if you don't know something
- listen carefully to the questions you are asked and don't be afraid to ask for clarification if you're not sure about something
- be prepared to give specific examples from your previous school or work experience of your own skills and qualities
- ensure that you achieve a normal amount of eye contact with your interviewers.

Your tasks

1 Select three job advertisements from the leisure and travel trade press, excluding any which are for retail travel consultants, which you think might be open to a school or college leaver. You should ensure that at least one advertisement is for a vacancy in the travel and tourism industry, and that one is in the leisure and recreation industry.

Write to each of the contact addresses provided and ask for further details.

2 On the basis of the information provided select the job that most appeals to you and create a Person and Role Profile for the post. You may find it useful to refer to the example provided in the text.

3 Review all the Person and Role Profiles produced by your group and agree which is the most interesting. Each student in the group should prepare and send letters and CVs applying for this position.

4 Appoint a panel to choose criteria which will be applied in short-listing candidates. This panel should select six candidates for interview.

5 Appoint an interviewing panel which should meet and agree the format of the interview, and how they will establish whether the skills and experience of the candidates matches the Person and Role Profile.

6 Conduct the six interviews with those not directly involved, making notes on both the approaches of the interviewing panel and on the performance of individual candidates.

7 Evaluate the performances of each panel and each individual applicant.

8 Repeat the tasks outlined in 2–7 for one of the other advertisements originally selected, ensuring that roles of panel members and selected applicants differ from the first time round.

(**Note:** One of the two exercises should relate to a travel and tourism vacancy and the other to a leisure and recreation vacancy.)

2.9 Staff appraisal

Develops knowledge and understanding of the following element:
2.4 Investigate workplace standards and performance in the leisure and tourism industries

Supports development of the following core skills:
Communication 3.2 (Task 1)
Communication 3.2, 3.4 (Task 2)

Evaluating the performance of individuals and teams at work can be carried out in a number of ways. Sometimes quantitative methods may be used. For example, the performance of a sales team can be measured in terms of the number and value of the sales they make. Personnel answering telephone enquiries can be assessed in terms of the number of calls they respond to and the average length of each call. Chefs can be assessed in terms of the time it takes to prepare a number of set menus.

Some work activities are difficult to assess in these terms, for example the quality of service in a restaurant or the effectiveness of the commentary given by a museum guide. Customer surveys may give some insight into the quality of service being provided, but many companies use a staff appraisal system to review the duties of individual employees and to see how effectively they are working with others. The system is used to judge how well each employee is performing and to identify their strengths and weaknesses. The process is not intended to focus on negative criticism, except where it is clearly deserved. The aim is to talk through each employee's current and potential contribution and to establish some future goals. This helps the company both in using each individual's potential and in matching them to work areas and work teams where they will flourish.

Evaluating individual and team performance in a restaurant.

Appraisal is generally carried out by means of an interview between the employee and their supervisor or head of department. Often a standard form is used, listing a number of questions for the head of department to answer about the employee's work performance. It will draw attention to accomplishments, difficulties and ability to work with others. Judgement about the individual's attitudes is usually asked for, including their knowledge of their duties and of company rules and regulations and of their response to company initiatives. The process usually involves the employee working with the supervisor to agree the levels of performance they have achieved in various aspects of the job during the appraisal period. They will also agree future objectives.

There is a risk that this system will make employees feel as if they are being treated like children. To try and avoid giving the impression that appraisal is like an examination in which failure is unforgivable, many companies also use an employer appraisal form. This gives employees the opportunity to say whether their duties have been clearly explained to them and whether they think they are ideally suited to the tasks they are performing or the teams they are working with. It gives the company the chance to find out the factors which most encourage and most discourage their work force. It is often a means of identifying problems and obstacles which have not previously come to light. It can also give indications of where more experience or training would increase effectiveness. In some firms appraisal is used as a means of assessing suitability for promotion or as a means of deciding the rate of annual salary increase.

In jobs where some kind of management function is involved a job description is likely to have been provided at the time of appointment. These are valuable in appraisal since they provide criteria against which to measure performance. They will also in time show which areas of the company's business are changing and so demanding more or less staff time spent on them.

Your tasks

1 List the different skills and qualities which you think ought to be regularly appraised in the following jobs:
- a museum guide
- a judo coach
- a pastry chef
- a coach driver
- a hotel receptionist.

2 Select one person currently employed in one of these five occupations. Use appropriate research methods to establish which other personnel they are required to work with.

Suggest an appraisal system designed to evaluate how well the personnel you have identified work as a team.

2.10 Visitor attractions: a national code of practice

Develops knowledge and understanding of the following element:
2.4 Investigate workplace standards and performance in the leisure and tourism industries

Supports development of the following core skills:
Application of number 3.1; Information Technology 3.1, 3.3 (Task 1)
Communication 3.2 (Task 2)

One difficulty in evaluating the performance of one tourism facility as opposed to that of another is the lack of agreed standards by which to judge them. In an effort to remedy this the English Tourist Board's Visitor Attractions Advisory Committee has drawn up a National Code of Practice. The purpose of the standards described in this code is both to safeguard the interests of the public and to reassure the tourist boards of the quality of the attractions they are including in regional and national promotions.

The Code begins by defining a visitor attraction in the following way:

A permanently established excursion destination, a primary purpose of which is to allow public access for entertainment, interest or education; rather than being a primary retail outlet or a venue for a sporting, theatrical, or film performances. It must be open to the public, without prior booking, for published periods each year, and should be capable of attracting day visitors or tourists, as well as local residents.

Attractions which conform to this definition can register their agreement to observe the Code and their performance against its standards are then monitored by the relevant regional tourist board. Attractions which do not register are not included in promotions and publications produced by the English Tourist Board. Registration entitles individual attractions both to display a certificate indicating the standards they are observing and to use a logo indicating that they participate in the scheme.

The National Code of Practice places an obligation on owners and managers of visitor attractions to fulfil requirements in seven areas. The first relates to the quality of information provided about the attraction. The code stipulates that it should be accurate and comprehensive. A particular concern relates to any specific conditions of entry. Potential visitors should know in advance if appointments are required or if children are not admitted. If parts of the attraction would be physically inaccessible to the very old or the very young, this should be made clear. Information about the site should not mislead. For example it should be clear which parts of the attraction allow free admission and which incur an entry charge. Publicity material should include clear directions about how to get to and from the attraction.

The second clause in the Code relates to entry charges. These should be clearly displayed at all entrances and should not disguise additional charges. It would not be realistic to list all the prices of food outlets and individual facilities at the entrance to large attractions, but the Code requires an acknowledgement at the entrance of the principle that such charges are made. Special charges agreed with visiting parties should be confirmed in writing so that the group leaders can bring written evidence of these agreed rates with them on the day of their visit.

The standards of customer care are highlighted by a requirement to ensure the safety, comfort and service of customers. Attractions must be clean. They must display adequate safety information and ensure that visitors receive good guidance. Equipment and facilities have to be maintained to a high standard, as well as being checked to see that they are fit for the purpose for which they are being used.

The National Code of Practice looks for a willingness to provide access for all people, whatever their needs.

On-site facilities will vary according to the size of the attraction. The Code makes reference to toilets, coach and car parking and catering arrangements. These should, as far as possible, meet the likely demand. Signing should make them easy to find and, where these facilities are not available, publicity material should indicate this.

The Code looks for a willingness on the part of attractions to provide access for all people, whatever their particular needs. It is perhaps the one standard where evaluation requires a degree of common sense. It is very difficult, for example, for the owners of underground cave systems or owners of some historic buildings to provide complete access for wheelchair users.

Any enquiries or complaints which are received should be dealt with quickly and courteously, regardless of whether they are spoken or written. If visitors do complain, the cause of their grievance should be properly investigated and where it is found to be reasonable they should be informed about what corrective action has been taken.

The final clause in the Code requires owners and managers to provide public liability insurance or, in Government owned properties, a comparable arrangement. Attractions should also abide by all other statutory regulations which apply to them. These might relate to such things as planning or health and safety.

Any registered attraction which is found not to be conforming with these seven requirements is first notified by the English Tourist Board. If the failure is not put right the attraction is withdrawn from the register and hence from any publicity or promotions of the national or regional tourist boards. Owners and managers who feel the original notification to be unjust, can submit evidence to an Appeals Panel which will give a final decision on the basis of the evidence and sometimes on a visit to the attraction.

Your tasks

1   Draw up a questionnaire which could be used as a guide by inspectors appointed by a regional tourist board to judge how effectively a visitor attraction was achieving the standards described in the Visitor Attraction National Code of Practice.

2   Make a tour of a visitor attraction in your own region and complete your questionnaire on the basis of what you observe there.

3   How many of the seven standards could be used in the following, each of which was excluded from the ETB's definition of visitor attractions:
   * a travelling fairground
   * an enclosed shopping mall
   * an athletics stadium
   * a cinema?

4   List other clauses which you think would need to be incorporated into a Code of Practice designed to assist in the evaluation of each of the four examples given in task 3.

2.11 Company quality assessment schemes

Develops knowledge and understanding of the following element:
2.4   Investigate workplace standards and performance in the leisure and tourism industries

Supports development of the following core skills:
Application of number 3.1, 3.3; Communication 3.1 (Task 1)
Communication 3.2 (Task 2)

Successful leisure and tourism companies usually aim both to retain their existing markets and to secure new ones. A major factor in achieving this is to guarantee the quality of the product or service being offered. In the past evaluation of business quality was often done internally and so gave little indication of the company's performance in relation to its competitors. The British Standards Institute Quality Assurance scheme offers industry the chance to have its products and quality systems assessed independently. Achieving BSI certification is an indication to customers that certain agreed quality standards have been met.

The BSI scheme which measures the overall quality standard of companies is known as BS 5750. It involves a team of assessors who first look at the quality system in operation already. They inspect all the documentation which sets out the quality standards and how they are achieved in the organisation being assessed. Companies which consistently produce goods to national standards can be licensed by BSI to use the BSI Kitemark on them, indicating their quality to potential purchasers. Service industries can use individual schemes to check the quality of aspects of their operations. For example the Call Routing Apparatus Maintenance scheme ensures that all equipment connected to the national telephone network is properly maintained.

The general quality standards which make up BS 5750 can be applied to individual sectors of industry. A process of consultation results in the drawing up of Quality Assessment Guides which are used in applying BS 5750 to the particular process or service under consideration. Leisure and tourism companies seeking this kind of quality certification would need this kind of consultation, not least because their products are far less tangible than those of a manufacturing company.

The areas which would come under scrutiny include the management of the company. Staff held responsible for quality standards should be seen to have the power to make improvements. The means by which they check efficiency and good service should be well defined and understood by all employees. Communication of the company's quality standards is generally initiated through induction training and supported by means of manuals relevant to the different departments and operations within the organisation. American Express, for example, provides a pack for all its business and retail travel centres, setting the standards of customer service which the company expects. The standards cover telephones, reservations, documentation, customer service and appearance. Some of these standards, for example the time from receipt of a ticket to processing it, are measured on a weekly basis and the results are aggregated to give an indication of performance across all American Express travel centres.

The quality of documentation within a company can be a measure of its efficiency. It affects both its internal communication and awareness, as well as the impression it creates outside. Good records generally mean fewer mistakes and time saved by needless duplication. Leisure and tourism companies often buy in services from other companies, such as caterers, designers or public relations specialists. Setting criteria for the suppliers of these services and setting up a system to monitor the quality of what they contribute should also form part of any quality assessment.

Maintaining quality in adverse circumstances can be a major test for any company. Good organisations try not to resort to crisis management. They attempt to plan for contingencies so that, for example, in the event of the absence of staff with specific responsibilities others are equipped to deputise without significantly reducing the effectiveness of what is being done. Where things do go wrong there should be an agreed corrective process. For some problems this will require a full investigation and a means of communicating effectively what preventative measures have been taken as a result.

Quality assessment, particularly in an organisation like a leisure centre, should also include a review of how relevant laws and regulations are made known and implemented. Safety issues relating to the handling of materials, the use of equipment and first aid training will have special significance in some leisure and tourism contexts. Training and regular checks are necessary to ensure that awareness of these issues and all others relating to quality is continuous.

Your tasks

1 A large travel agency branch office employing six travel counsellors decides to monitor its telephone calls from customers. The manager selects a random half hour each week when all incoming calls are checked. The following information is noted: how long it took to answer the call; how long the call lasted; how many calls were lost.

Discuss how useful you think the data which was gathered as a result of this monitoring would be in judging the quality of service being offered by the agency.

2 Collect a number of examples of items sold as souvenirs at tourist attractions. Draw up a plan which would enable the makers to evaluate the quality of their products.

Unit 3 Marketing in leisure and tourism

3.1 Pricing decisions in leisure facilities

Develops knowledge and understanding of the following element:
3.1 Investigate marketing principles, activities and objectives in leisure and tourism

Supports development of the following core skills:
Communication 3.2, 3.4 (Task 1)
Communication 3.2, 3.3 (Task 2)
Application of number 3.2 (Task 3)
Communication 3.2 (Task 4)

What factors determine price?

Deciding how much to charge for admission to a leisure facility is not easy. The facility needs to make enough money to ensure that it can meet its costs. Some of the costs may be paid for by a local authority. Where this is the case, the facility will have to make sure that its prices ensure it is attracting a sufficiently wide spectrum of the local community.

A number of different factors will determine the pricing policy employed by a leisure facility. The most important ones are as follows.

- Is the facility expected to run at a profit?
- Does it receive any subsidies?
- How variable is the demand for use of the facility?
- What kind of costs does the facility have to meet?
- What are people willing to pay for the use of both other similar facilities and other alternative recreational activities?
- What do competitors charge?

Three examples of how specific leisure facilities set their prices

1 Swindon Town Football Club
Prices vary depending on which part of the ground supporters are admitted to. As with most clubs, new stands with improved facilities and viewing positions near the half-way line will be priced more highly than seats with limited views or which are not under cover.

First of all the club looks at the previous season's prices, taking account also of whether the team is in the same division. Promotion would mean better opposition and a consideration of price increases. Relegation would mean looking carefully at what fans would consider value for money for watching the team play weaker opposition. There are more price controls in the Premier League than outside it. In the First Division Swindon ran a 'Quid-a-kid' scheme. This encourages families to attend games and introduces a new generation of potential fans to the sport.

Gate prices are set at the start of the season so that season ticket holders know what savings they will make. An additional benefit for those buying season tickets is that they rarely have to queue for admission.

2 Thamesdown Borough Council leisure facilities

Overall prices are influenced most by the budget set for Thamesdown Leisure. The aim of the Council's Leisure Management Committee is to set prices which meet the majority of costs but will still appeal to customers. In other words, prices must not be raised to a level where local people cease to use facilities altogether.

A discount scheme is offered for daytime use to those who are unemployed, or who are senior citizens, or who are receiving State benefits of some kind. The existence of this kind of discount often indicates that the pricing policy has been influenced by the political views of whichever party has a majority on the Council.

Individual facilities, such as the swimming pool at the Rec, offer season tickets to frequent users. The cost of a season ticket for swimmers is the equivalent of the cost of 25 individual sessions, so that anyone in possession of a season ticket who uses the pool more than 25 times gains a financial benefit.

Facilities are intended mainly for the use of borough residents. There is no membership scheme as this might exclude some local groups. Identity cards enable facilities such as squash courts to be booked in advance. However, those living inside the borough can book seven days in advance, while those living outside can only book six days in advance. This means local residents tend to get priority where facilities are in great demand.

Occasionally special promotional prices are introduced in order to attract more visitors, especially outside peak hours. For example, the Rec Swimming Pool recently offered six swimming sessions for the price of five.

3 Colley's Supper Rooms, Lechlade, Gloucestershire

There is a set price for menus from Monday to Thursday. However, prices rise on Friday and Saturday nights since these are easily the most popular nights for eating out.

Discounts are offered at different times of year between January and September. These vary from flat-rate discounts of up to 10 per cent to offers of four meals for the price of three. Decisions about the types of promotion to be offered are taken in the preceding month and will depend mainly on how many forward reservations have been received.

Holding prices fairly steady is important in encouraging repeat visits. Although the costs of different foodstuffs may vary considerably at different times of year, large price increases can be avoided by choosing menus which avoid excessively costly ingredients.

Low prices

From the user's point of view, the lowest prices possible would appear to be a very attractive feature for a leisure facility. Indeed low prices are often used as a means of trying to attract people to new facilities which are attempting to establish themselves and draw people away from their competitors. Prices may be reduced in existing facilities in order to try to attract new market groups or to encourage more visitors during off-peak times. There are two main disadvantages of low prices. They may reduce the amount of revenue the facility attracts and this in turn will affect the quality of the service it can provide. It will be able to employ fewer staff, and spend less on maintenance and refurbishment than a facility with a higher income. A facility which consistently charges low prices may come to be regarded as cheap and this may limit its ability to attract more users.

High prices

Leisure facilities sometimes choose to set higher than average prices. The main purpose of such a policy is to establish an exclusive atmosphere. This is often reinforced by a 'members only' policy. It is based on the belief that people in higher income brackets will be attracted, but it also means that the facility will have to commit itself to delivering a product which is of higher than average quality if it is to retain these more demanding members.

Variable prices

Most leisure facilities vary their prices either for different customer groups or for different times of day. For example discounts may be offered to senior citizens, young children, school groups or unemployed people. These rates are most frequently available at times when the facility is least used, such as mornings or afternoons in the middle of the week. The highest prices charged where a variable price policy applies are likely to be at times when the facility is in greatest demand, such as weekdays or evenings.

The same principle often applies to theatre or music performances where tickets for the most popular shows will cost more than those for others. Some professional football clubs have recently introduced differential pricing policies. This means that ticket prices vary according to the quality of the opposition. Spectators have to pay more to see games against teams at the top of the league or with star players.

Special prices

The majority of leisure facilities have pricing systems which mainly depend on cash payments on admission. Those which are venues for sports or arts performances will generally have advanced booking arrangements, whereby tickets can be purchased or reserved ahead of the date they are issued for. A ticket system is often run alongside schemes which offer special prices to those who attend the facility regularly. Reductions may be made available to those who buy season tickets entitling them to watch a whole sequence of football matches or a season of plays at a theatre. The benefit to the facility is that this guarantees them some income, regardless of whether the purchaser attends all the performances. It also provides them with cash in advance, which may help them to meet their running costs.

Leisure centre membership schemes have the same advantage. The income is guaranteed however frequently the member attends. It also reduces the amount of administration and security required when every user of the centre stops at reception to pay cash on entry. For the same reasons, theme parks often make a single charge at the main entrance rather than charging separately for each different ride visitors use.

Special prices are also used as a means of promoting new activities at existing facilities. Special offers may be used to encourage existing members to introduce their friends to the facility. These offers may take the form of free gifts, temporary free membership for guests or short-term trial membership at considerably reduced rates.

Your tasks

The Haydon Leisure Centre can be hired for children's parties. At the moment four party packages are available. This is how the leaflet advertising them describes what is offered.

Birthday Party Package for YOU!

It's the greatest way to hold a children's party. No need to worry about noisy children at your home. No need to say 'Watch the carpet!' Why not bring the noise and mayhem to the Haydon Centre and get the most out of our Party Packages!

PARTY PACKAGE 1
Full use of the Flexi Hall (sports hall), to play and organise your own games at an incredible Price of £15.60.

PARTY PACKAGE 2
Full use of the Flexi Hall, plus a member of staff to organise and supervise a variety of fun-packed activities and games. Price £20.60

PARTY PACKAGE 3
Full use of the Flexi Hall plus the Centre's own bouncy castle – a real crowd puller! Price £25.60*

PARTY PACKAGE 4
For a 'Mega-Party' this package has got the lot! Fun and games in the Flexi Hall plus the bouncy castle and a member of staff to arrange and supervise fun activities and games. This is the party everyone wants to be invited to and all for the Price of £30.60*

* For Party Packages 3 and 4 the bouncy castle must be erected and dismantled within the period of your booking.

The Centre has received a number of requests for additional party packages, including demands for (a) longer sessions, (b) more than one staff member and (c) use of a junior swimming pool.

1 List the marketing objectives the centre might adopt in broadening the scope of its activities for young children.

2 Write descriptions of three new party packages which the Haydon Centre could offer.

3 Suggest a price for each package, explaining why you have arrived at these figures.

4 List any factors which you think would lead the centre to considering changing its prices for any of the party packages it offers.

3.2 The role of promotion in marketing leisure facilities

Develops knowledge and understanding of the following element:
3.1 Investigate marketing principles, activities and objectives in leisure and tourism

Supports development of the following core skills:
Communication 3.2, 3.4 (Task 1)
Communication 3.1 (Task 2)
Application of number 3.2; Communication 3.2 (Task 3)
Communication 3.2 (Task 4)

The purpose of promotion

Promotion is used to give potential customers an idea of what goes on in a leisure facility, both in terms of the range of activities and services it offers, and the atmosphere which is created inside it. Demand for many leisure facilities is seasonal and promotion is needed to stimulate sales during off-peak periods. There is a wide range of leisure activities which customers can choose to take up. They may choose to do without leisure activities altogether when economic conditions are hard. Both these factors make promotion essential for leisure companies wishing to stave off the competition.

Promotion of a leisure facility is concerned with communicating its range of services to targeted market segments. The table below summarises the most common ways in which a facility might do this.

Advertising	Local and national newspapers, magazines, trade press, posters, hoardings, bus sides, local and national radio, television, direct mail
Sales promotion	Point of sale material, prizes, price discounts, promotional evenings, in-store promotional events, branding of products
Publicity and public relations	Press visits, press releases, special events, product placement in film and TV programme locations, community projects and charity donations

Advertising

The basic aim of any advertisement is to stimulate enough interest to persuade people to become customers. The type of advertising chosen and the medium used depends on the target audience. Since leisure facilities are often seeking to attract local residents, they often choose to advertise through the medium of the local press or local radio. Another reason for choosing local media is cost. Advertising on television or in the national press might enable them to reach a wider audience but these are also the most expensive of the media.

Advertising for leisure facilities will generally focus on one of the following approaches:

- stressing price in relation to competitors, e.g. discounts
- stressing extra value over competitors' products, e.g. range of flumes and wave machines at a swimming pool
- stressing the uniqueness of the product, e.g. the only bowling alley in town.

Sales promotion

The purpose of sales promotion is usually to generate immediate sales. A pub offering cheap drinks during a 'happy hour' is hoping to attract additional cash customers during normally quiet periods. Sales promotion, therefore, often has more short-term objectives than advertising.

Sales promotions are common in the leisure and tourism industry. Examples include the habit of some restaurants of offering a free bottle of wine with meals over a certain price or pubs offering free 'live' music performances on certain nights of the week. Sometimes promotions are jointly launched with companies outside leisure and tourism. These may encourage consumers to buy extra retail goods for the vouchers which accompany them. For example chocolate bars may carry vouchers which can be redeemed against items like the cost of admission to cinema performances.

Publicity and public relations

The public reputation of a facility will almost certainly affect its business performance, even though this may be hard to measure. Good public relations is not just about the facility's relationship with its customers. It should include their suppliers, other companies with which they do business, trade organisations and regulatory bodies, professional associations and trade unions, the local community, public figures and the news media.

One essential difference between public relations (often referred to as PR) and advertising is that other people often see advertising as biased, while other kinds of publicity seem more impartial. The information provided about a leisure facility by a visiting journalist or television reporter is regarded as the view of an outsider with no reason to provide only favourable comments.

Good press relations are important if any leisure facility hopes to gain regular coverage of its activities. It takes time to build a good reputation and the sustaining of good press relations is important to the facility's long-term objectives. A good relationship helps the facility understand what makes a good news story. It may also help in emphasising the good publicity it receives and playing down any potentially harmful publicity, such as vandalism or theft at the facility.

Choosing the right methods of promotion

Choosing which methods of promotion to use will depend on the intended target market, the overall marketing objectives and the marketing budget.

Promotion can take a number of forms, not all of which involve working through the media. Restaurants, for example, are often faced with the problem of considerably fewer diners on Mondays and Tuesdays than later in the week. There are several strategies they can adopt to try and counter this. They can:

- run special evenings to celebrate festivals such as Easter or May Day
- put on themed events associated with occasions like Valentine's Day, Guy Fawkes' Night or Hallowe'en

- design menus based on seasons of the year, local festivals or local famous people
- promote evenings featuring the cuisine and perhaps music of other countries.

This type of promotion can be advertised by local posters, a press release to the local newspaper and perhaps the distribution of leaflets to households in the immediate vicinity.

The chosen method of promotion will reflect the budget available. If the budget is small, the chosen method of promotion may be the production and limited distribution of inexpensive leaflets, perhaps produced in-house on a photocopier. Larger budgets are needed if the medium is more expensive, such as a glossy brochure, or if distribution of promotional material is more widespread.

Examples of promotional activities by leisure facilities

A professional football club can promote its name through the sale of leisure wear and other items bearing the club's logo. Promotion is often a two-way process for professional sports with a high profile. Live television coverage means that other companies will pay the host club to position advertisements at strategic points around the ground.

Garden centres will often mount promotions with companies whose products they sell. For example, Kennedy's Garden Centres recently worked jointly with Fisons to promote both the sale of hanging baskets and the plant food which Fisons recommend for feeding these baskets.

Leisure facilities often used computerised booking systems to generate address lists which they can use for direct mail promoting new products or services. Sports centres may use this process to advertise leisure goods which they offer for sale in a retail centre.

Cinemas and theatres will generally advertise in the local press. They may also pay to have information about dates and times of performances listed in weekly entertainments guides, and on television information systems like Ceefax and Prestel. Journalists may be invited to new plays and film premières in the hope that they will give wider coverage by writing reviews of what they have seen. This can backfire of course if the reviews are not very complimentary!

Your tasks

Read the advertisement on page 62, taken from a Wasps Rugby Football Club programme.

1 Explain what you think are the advantages to each of the two participants in this promotion.

2 Choose a leisure facility you have visited and propose three local companies involved in different types of business which the facility might think about approaching with ideas of joint promotions.

3 Briefly explain the aims of three possible promotions which the facility might consider putting to the companies concerned, and the main terms they would offer in order to persuade people or companies to become involved.

4 Make a list of the questions you think the companies concerned would wish to have answered before they agreed to take part in such joint promotions.

Help Your Business Take Flight – Join The Fly Half Club

THE FLY HALF CLUB is a new initiative developed by Wasps Rugby Club Promotions Ltd in partnership with United Airlines, for forward thinking companies who are keen to associate with high flyers.

Inspired by the quality of the player at the number 10 position, here are ten of the best reasons to join:-

1. Corporate membership of Wasps – four reserved seats at every home game – ability to apply for International tickets plus many other benefits.

2. Complimentary membership of The Rugby Club of London, a private dining club in the West End.

3. Entry into a draw to win a day out for four at a Five Nations Championship match at Twickenham.

4. A series of occasional events and dinners throughout the year.

5. Discounts on Club merchandise.

6. Two free tickets on United Airlines to any of five US gateways.

7. Membership of United Airlines' Mileage Plus Scheme plus 5000 free air miles.

8. Access to United Airlines' Red Carpet Club at Heathrow.

9. Two free days car hire with Eurodollar rent-a-car and 20% discount off the UK business tariff.

10. 25% discount on accommodation at the Forum Hotel, London and 10% off food and beverage on restaurant and conference bookings.

SPECIAL REDUCED MID-SEASON MEMBERSHIP FEE £1,000!

PICK UP A BROCHURE TODAY FROM THE BAR AREAS OR CALL SARA RIGBY, MARKETING MANAGER, FOR AN INFORMAL CHAT

3.3 Satisfying the visitor: market research

Develops knowledge and understanding of the following element:

3.2 Analyse and undertake market research in leisure and tourism organisations

Supports development of the following core skills:

Application of number 3.3; Communication 3.1 (Task 1)
Application of number 3.3 (Task 2)
Application of number 3.3; Communication 3.2 (Task 3)

Most visitor attractions carry out market research by distributing questionnaires to people as they leave. These are often referred to as exit surveys. The data gathered is generally incorporated into a memorandum for all departments, showing how the statistics compare with past performance and offering a comment on the trends revealed and their likely significance.

At a visitor attraction, much of the data may relate to different physical areas, sometimes using a simple rating system which asks visitors to judge how enjoyable or satisfactory they found separate features. Some surveys begin by asking visitors to indicate from a specific list of facilities the ones they expected to find before they arrived. This type of question provides the attraction with information about the general awareness which the public has of it and how accurate this is. It may reveal that some of their facilities are not well known, or that ideas of what to expect have changed over a number of years.

Providing food outlets at a major attraction requires some market research to establish whether the range and quality of the service is what customers want. Research at Churchett Hall, for example, might have shown the following:

Whether food was brought	1989 %	1990 %	1991 %	1992 %
picnic	40	38	37	36
some snacks/drinks	19	24	26	33
no picnic/other food	41	38	37	31

This showed that the proportion of visitors bringing their own snacks was rising. The marketing department would have to consider why this was. It could be that prices at existing food outlets were regarded as high, or it could be simply that people spend less money during a recession. A further question, however, might have revealed that those who did use the food outlets judged the quality of the facilities to be very good.

Data about previous visits is particularly important in leisure and tourism. Not only are repeat visits vital to economic survival, but they also represent a previously satisfied market. Customers are already informed about what they are coming to and technically less money has had to be spent on advertising in order to attract them.

Suppose that research at two contrasting attractions showed the following patterns of repeat visits:

Number of previous visits to Churchett Hall (%)	1989 %	1990 %	1991 %	1992 %
none	52	44	54	45
one	21	24	15	14
two or three	17	20	20	28
four or more	6	12	10	13

Number of previous visits to Aylott Park (%)	1990 %	1991 %	1992 %
none	36	28	25
one or more	64	72	75

These figures show a rise in the proportion of repeat visitors to Churchett Hall and Aylott Park. The two sets of data show some of the difficulties of drawing comparisons:
- figures for 1989 are not available for both attractions
- questions in the surveys asked the respondents to discriminate differently about the number of their previous visits.

This means, for example, that it is possible to conclude from these figures that three quarters of the visitors to Aylott Park have been once before, but it is also possible that the same proportion have all been three times before. When viewing this data you should also take into consideration points such as the location of the two attractions and the radius from within which they attract the majority of their visitors. Suppose the journey times to the two attractions were as shown in the following tables:

Journey time to Churchett Hall	1988 %	1989 %	1990 %	1991 %	1992 %
0–½ hour	36	36	33	33	25
1½ hour	34	35	37	37	38
1–½ hours	20	17	18	17	21
1½–2 hours	9	9	9	10	13
2 hours or more	1	1	3	3	3

Journey time to Aylott Park 1992 (groups only)	
	%
0–1 hour	23
1–½ hours	29
1½–2 hours	32
2–2½ hours	12
2½ hours or more	4

Again the data is reported in a slightly different way which restricts the amount of direct comparison. There is a clear trend showing that more visitors are coming to Churchett Hall from further afield. However, Aylott Park still has a wider geographical appeal, with a much higher proportion of visitors travelling for more than two hours to get there.

Market research surveys may ask respondents about their television viewing habits, the newspapers they read or whether they listen regularly to commercial radio. The purpose of such questions is to establish the most appropriate **media** for future advertising campaigns. Similarly a question which establishes profiles of visitors, by age and social class for example, indicates which markets the attraction is successfully penetrating.

Your tasks

Study the following table about the types of parties visiting a popular leisure park:

	1989 %	1990 %	1991 %	1992 %
individual/'on my own'	0	0	0	3
adults without children	19	22	32	38
one parent with children	12	10	9	9
both parents with children	42	35	27	25
2 or more women with children	7	3	6	5
other adult(s) with child(ren)	20	30	26	20

1 Discuss the trends that can be identified from this data.

2 Give possible explanations for the trends you have found.

3 Write a short memorandum for all departments within the leisure park suggesting what implications these figures might have for 1993.

3.4 Marketing tourism: information technology

Develops knowledge and understanding of the following element:
3.2 Analyse and undertake marketing research in leisure and tourism organisations

Supports development of the following core skills:
Application of number 3.3 (Task 1)
Application of number 3.3 (Task 2)

Computing and telecommunications have already made a significant impact on leisure and tourism, especially in the travel industry. Computers have been used for some time to store such information as airline seat availability and prices. Sophisticated computer reservations systems (often known simply as CRS) like Sabre can store as many as 50 million fares and handle over 2000 transactions per second. Travel agents can make bookings in a fraction of the time it used to take when they had to telephone airlines and tour operators for basic information. The development of advanced telecommunications systems also means that sales and marketing information can be **networked** to sales staff and customers around the world extremely rapidly.

Tourism businesses may not, however, always be in a position to take advantage of these developments. Placing information about a business or a tourist destination or service on a CRS is expensive. The development costs can be high and charges are made to those doing business through the systems. The provision of data for a CRS is in any case only a part of the marketing process: it does not guarantee that the customers who might be interested in purchasing the product actually get to see the information about it. Nor does it guarantee they will buy it even if they do get access to the right information. Placing information about your business on a CRS also hands a degree of control over bookings and purchases to other users of the system, such as travel agents. Owners of small businesses may in particular be reluctant to give up altogether their control over the type of custom they attract.

Destinations such as seaside resorts with large numbers of small guest houses and self-catering apartments might find that their range of accommodation was less successfully represented on CRSs than destinations with many large international hotels. So counter staff in travel agents outside the immediate area might find that they had more access to information about resorts with large international hotels than to those with small guest houses and self-catering apartments.

According to Gilbert Archdale, writing in the Tourism Society's bulletin, the answer to the problem of destinations wishing to maintain their share of the market despite their dependence on small tourism businesses lies with destination databases. These would link the existing databases of products, like tours and attractions, with databases containing customer information and with CRSs. It would help the travel agent to establish a swift and automatic link between the customers' interests and needs and the most suitable destinations. Without such developments there is every chance that holiday choices will continue to be controlled by tour operators and airlines.

65

The information in the following tables is taken from market analysis prepared by a company called CCN Marketing Ltd for use by the Co-op Travelcare Service. It deals with some of the leisure activities of the residents of the towns of Rhyl and Abingdon.

Information Technology has been used to analyse data taken from, among other sources, the National Census. Computer calculations enable the figures for Rhyl and Abingdon to be compared rapidly with the national totals (referred to as the base).

The third pair of columns is perhaps of most interest to marketing departments. The concept of penetration offers them a means of assessing the extent to which a known group of people differs from the average. This can be applied to their knowledge of a product or, as in this case, to aspects of their tastes and lifestyles. The last column in these two tables (the index) shows whether the proportion of residents taking part in each leisure activity is higher or lower than the national average.

Analysis of the leisure activities of the residents of Rhyl

Title: Leisure data
Target zone: 5 km radius of Rhyl

Client: Co-operative Wholesale Society
Base zone: Great Britain (national)

	Target zone		Base zone		Target/base	
	Count	Ratio	Count	Ratio	Penetration	Index
Household data						
Total 1989 households	15 519	100.0%	22 012 432	100%	0.00071	100
Holidays						
Beach/resort holiday last year	3300	21.3%	4 806 745	21.8%	0.00069	97
2 or more holidays last year	4212	27.1%	5 823 388	26.5%	0.00072	103
Last holiday less than £250	4332	27.9%	6 010 680	27.3%	0.00072	102
Last holiday more than £1000	829	5.3%	1 227 426	5.6%	0.00068	96
Flown in the last 3 years	6928	44.6%	9 424 961	42.8%	0.00074	104
Population data						
Total 1989 population	38 483	100.0%	55 310 568	100.0%	0.00070	100
Social activities						
Visit restaurants once a month	4512	11.7%	6 633 672	12.0%	0.00068	98
Visit pubs 2–3 times a week	5148	13.4%	7 740 843	14.0%	0.00067	96
Play bingo at club regularly	2218	5.8%	3 700 292	6.7%	0.00060	86
Keep fit regularly	3845	10.0%	49 960 84	9.0%	0.00077	111
Television viewing						
Watch American football	5274	13.7%	7 856 216	14.2%	0.00067	96
Watch soccer	11 128	28.9%	16 959 980	30.7%	0.00066	94
Watch cricket	9196	23.9%	12 839 606	23.2%	0.00072	103
Watch horse racing	4909	12.8%	7 129 368	12.9%	0.00069	99
Watch wrestling	5440	14.1%	8 291 222	15.0%	0.00066	94

Analysis of the leisure activities of the residents of Abingdon

Title: Leisure data

Client: Co-operative Wholesale Society

Target zone: 5 km radius of Abingdon

Base zone: Great Britain (target)

	Target zone		Base zone		Target/base	
	Count	Ratio	Count	Ratio	Penetration	Index
Household data						
Total 1989 households	19 309	100.0%	22 013 696	100%	0.00088	100
Holidays						
Beach/resort holiday last year	4571	23.7%	4 806 986	21.8%	0.00095	108
2 or more holidays last year	5985	31.0%	5 823 783	26.5%	0.00103	117
Last holiday less than £250	5427	28.1%	60 110 53	27.3%	0.00090	103
Last holiday more than £1000	1455	7.5%	1 227 516	5.6%	0.00119	135
Flown in the last 3 years	9425	48.8%	9 425 585	42.8%	0.00100	114
Population data						
Total 1989 population	53 164	100.0%	55 313 668	100.0%	0.00096	100
Social activities						
Visit restaurants once a month	7412	13.9%	66 340 67	12.0%	0.00112	116
Visit pubs 2–3 times a week	7238	13.6%	7 741 248	14.0%	0.00093	97
Play bingo at club regularly	2337	4.4%	3 700 410	6.7%	0.00063	66
Keep fit regularly	4972	9.4%	4996352	9.0%	0.00100	104
Television viewing						
Watch American football	7926	14.9%	7 856 617	14.2%	0.00101	105
Watch soccer	15 820	29.8%	16 960 932	30.7%	0.00093	97
Watch cricket	13 219	24.9%	12 840 417	23.2%	0.00103	107
Watch horse racing	6084	11.4%	7 129 734	12.9%	0.00085	89
Watch wrestling	7216	13.6%	8 291 590	15.0%	0.00087	91

1 A company is planning to open a new sports and leisure complex and has decided that Rhyl or Abingdon might be potentially profitable sites. What evidence could they use from this data to support the choice of one town or the other as the more suitable?

2 A travel agent has offices in Rhyl and Abingdon and is considering promotions of the following holidays in both branches:
- a budget Greek island 'sun and sand' holiday in June
- a 3-month round the world luxury cruise
- a 'first child free' offer for a week at a UK holiday camp in September
- a trip to Ireland to watch the Irish Grand National
- a 10-day gourmet tour of France.

Using data from the analysis, how could you best advise the agent as to which holiday to promote in each town?

67

3.5 Marketing *A Day at the Wells*

Develops knowledge and understanding of the following element:

3.3   Investigate and evaluate marketing communications in leisure and tourism organisations

Supports development of the following core skills:

Communication 3.4 (Task 1)

Communication 3.4 (Task 2)

Communication 3.4 (Task 3)

Marketing an attraction is intended to increase its number of visitors and hence its revenue. In order to be successful it needs to convince potential visitors that the attraction is good value for money. Good marketing can also benefit the destination as a whole, attracting people from outside to spend money there.

A *Day at the Wells* is a tourist attraction in Tunbridge Wells. It consists of an exhibition in the town's renovated Corn Exchange, recreating a summer's day in the town as it might have been in 1740. There are scenes representing, among other things, a stage coach departure, a coffee house and a candlelit ball.

The first concern in marketing an attraction such as this is to identify the **target markets**. These might include:

- the travel trade
- ferry operators
- organisers of educational visits
- local residents
- groups with an interest in Georgian or local history
- local companies looking for interesting conference venues.

The next decision to be made is how best to communicate with these target markets. Though the best known means of doing this is by advertising, there are other ways of increasing public awareness of the attraction:

- good press and public relations can ensure coverage of events and new developments within the attraction
- joint promotions, run with companies like British Rail, may attract new visitors by offering special concessions
- being represented at trade exhibitions offers the attraction the opportunity to persuade tour operators to include it in the itinerary of some of their tours
- good signs in the local area mean that casual visitors to Tunbridge Wells are more likely to be drawn towards *A Day at the Wells*
- the use of costumed actors on the surrounding streets can arouse the curiosity of potential visitors.

A *Day at the Wells* is only one of a number of attractions marketed by a company called Heritage Projects. Others include *The Oxford Story, The Canterbury Tales,* and *The White Cliffs Experience.* Joint marketing of these attractions means that the same target markets can be reached more cost effectively. All of these attractions conduct exit surveys in order to find out more about the kind of people they are attracting. These surveys ask where visitors have come from, how they came to hear of the attraction, and what they thought of

Period costume on show at A Day at The Wells.

various aspects of their experience. Many of the questions are designed to produce short answers which will provide quantitative data. In other words, the attractions will be able to draw conclusions about such things as the percentage of visitors who come from within a radius of two hours' travelling time.

Most marketing departments will have a computer database of contacts and addresses for direct mail. These mean that the user can select the particular target market – for example, coach operators or schools – and only print out addresses to these. This is more cost effective than sending every promotion to all addresses on the database. Attractions will often use sophisticated analyses of residential areas in order to pinpoint the type of market they hope to reach. If *A Day at the Wells* decides that its main market is people in social income groups A, B, and C1 and old-age pensioners, most of them coming from the South East, it can pay a research company to come up with suggested clusters of housing likely to provide the highest concentration of such people.

The medium chosen and the style of communicating are also important. If exit surveys suggest that people visiting *A Day at the Wells* do so primarily for entertainment, leaflets and television advertising would reflect this fact by aiming at a relatively light-hearted approach. *The Oxford Story*, on the other hand, probably attracts more visitors seeking background information about the city's history, so this is reflected in leaflets advertising the attraction. *The White Cliffs Experience* did not attract many visitors in hot weather since it was seen solely as an indoor attraction. Yet it proved possible to extend its market by organising a programme of outdoor events there.

It is important to get the pricing policy right if visitors are to be persuaded to come to an attraction. There are several general relevant factors. Attractions like Chessington World of Adventures, whose main market is families with children aged up to 14, are aware that the price of admission needs to fall within most families' idea of a budget for a day out. Setting too high a cost for the whole family may mean that one parent will opt out of the visit and go for a stroll or a cup of tea! It may be that certain prices represent psychological barriers, so that though people are willing to pay £9.99 for something they will not pay over £10. Another factor in the pricing policy of an individual attraction will be charges made by competitors. It can either aim to undercut them, or to demonstrate that the attraction offers an experience of a higher quality which is worth paying more for. The overall economic climate will have a bearing too, in that it is more difficult to raise admission charges during a recession. Pricing will also depend on the policy of the attraction's owners. Where attractions have been partly funded by the local council, as with *The White Cliffs Experience*, or where some of the directors of a project are also local councillors, as with the Dome in Doncaster, the pricing policy will need to take account of the overall council strategy for the area.

Not all revenue from an attraction comes from admission charges. Retailing is increasingly used as a feature of indoor attractions like *A Day at the Wells*, offering gifts, local books and souvenirs as reminders of the visit. Some attractions employ active retailing. For example, at *The Tales of Robin Hood* visitors can have a lesson in firing a bow and arrow. They can then move on to a shop within the attraction where, among other items, bows and arrows are for sale.

Attractions like Chessington World of Adventures which use regional television advertising as their main means of promotion will also need to evaluate the effects of each campaign, to ensure that they are worth the investment. They employ an outside agency to conduct carefully structured interviews to test people's awareness of the advertisements shown. High recall of the content suggests the campaign is succeeding. Chessington would

---

Royal Tunbridge Wells' most elegant attraction
A Day at the Wells: a Georgian journey

Entertaining and educational, A Day at the Wells brilliantly recreates a summer's day in 1740, in the elegant and scandalous spa resort of Tunbridge Wells.

The exhibition, acclaimed for its authentic scenes and lifelike models, takes you on a journey into the past, starting from a coaching inn in Southwark where the stage coach is about to leave for Tunbridge Wells.

A typical day at 'the Wells' unfolds: a congenial coffee for gentlemen in the Coffee house; a stroll for the ladies along The Pantiles to see and be seen; a glass of the medicinal and aphrodisiac spring water said to cure almost everything, and a glamorous candlelit ball for which to prepare...

Commentaries

There is a special commentary for children and commentaries in foreign languages are available. Arrangements have been made for the hard of hearing.

Facilities for the disabled

We welcome visitors with impaired mobility and have access for wheelchairs. Please make an advance booking.

Group bookings

A Day at the Wells is perfect for group visits. A pre-booked group is offered a 10 per cent reduction on the normal admission price. Trade Manual and Group information are available on request.

Evening viewing can be arranged for groups and refreshments provided. A Day at the Wells holds an alcohol licence.

A spacious hospitality room provides facilities for conference delegates, corporate entertainment and special celebrations.

Gift shop

A separate shop offers a wonderful selection of individual gifts, local books and souvenirs.

Educational services

A Teachers' Resource Pack, containing suggestions for activities based on the exhibition, is available. Together with work based on historical topics and local studies, the pack suggests follow-up activities in English, Geography, Science, Maths, Technology and the Arts.

A fully equipped education room is available and our education officer is on site to give advice and help where necessary.

need to ensure that its adverts were shown between programmes likely to appeal especially to the 8-14 age group. Television advertising space can be purchased at different rates, mainly dependent on the anticipated number of viewers at the intended slot. A particular time can only be guaranteed if the highest rates are paid. At other times a potential advertiser can be pre-empted by someone offering a higher sum for the same slot.

Your tasks

Read the text from the leaflet advertising *A Day at the Wells* on the previous page and then answer the following questions:

1 How many different markets is the leaflet intended to appeal to?

2 What different techniques have been used to try to appeal to each of these different markets?

3 Find each of the following words used in the text:
brilliantly, elegant, scandalous, authentic, congenial, gentlemen, aphrodisiac, glamorous. Discuss why you think they were chosen instead of the following possible alternatives: charmingly, smart, offensive, genuine, sociable, men, love-inducing, exciting.

3.6 Beaulieu: marketing an attraction

Develops knowledge and understanding of the following element:
3.3 Investigate and evaluate marketing communications in leisure and tourism organisations

Supports development of the following core skills:
Communication 3.1, 3.4 (Task 1)

Beaulieu is a highly successful visitor destination, attracting some half a million visitors each year. It offers a range of facilities, the best known of which is the National Motor Museum. In addition visitors can see the remains of the 13th century Abbey and parts of the Palace House, the Montagu family home. At nearby Buckler's Hard, on the same family estate, there are a Maritime Museum and a number of historic cottages to see.

To market the attraction successfully detailed research is carried out and analysed. An automated ticketing system can generate some initial information about visitors, showing for example, that 62 per cent are adults, 29 per cent are children and the remainder are senior citizens. About 40 per cent of the visitors come in July and August, during the main school holiday period. In addition a random sample of visitors to Beaulieu is interviewed using a standard questionnaire. Awareness surveys are also carried out in towns up to 100 miles away to try to gauge the general public's perception of Beaulieu.

This research reveals that 70 per cent of Beaulieu's visitors are holiday-makers, while the remainder are making one day excursions from home. The nearby New Forest and the seaside resort of Bournemouth are the most common points of departure for the holiday visitors. About one third of the holiday-makers stay in hotels or guest houses and a further third are on camping or caravan sites. Half the visitors come in groups including children and about a third are adult couples.

On average visitors stay four hours at Beaulieu. Almost everyone visits the most popular feature, The National Motor Museum. Research also suggests that most visitors have seen some publicity for Beaulieu before their visit, either on television or through leaflets. Visitors completing the questionnaire also indicate both the level of enjoyment the visit generated and the extent to which they felt it was value for money.

Armed with this accurate information about its visitors, the Public Relations Department is able to identify its target market. They must be people who have an interest either in the particular combination of motor, maritime and architectural history or who are keenly interested in one of these areas. The research is also important in allocating the annual marketing budget.

Once the target market has been identified, a decision is needed about the type of medium which will be most likely to make an impact yet be acceptable in terms of the cost to the company. For example, a nationwide television campaign might increase the visitor numbers but might cost more than the income generated by these extra visitors. Alternative media – such as the press, radio, journals, posters, leaflets or panels on the sides of buses – might prove to be more cost effective.

One difficulty faced by all marketers of attractions is trying to decide on the particular image they wish to put across. The public may find it easier to visualise a zoo or an art gallery than to have a clear picture of a leisure park or a mixed attraction. Many attractions began with a single focus but have since added other major features, sometimes to the extent that the original focus has become the secondary interest: Beaulieu is still best known for the Motor Museum and this will tend to feature first in general publicity but the other attractions have to be given due weight as well. The aim of the marketing will be to maximise people's enjoyment and make them fully aware of all the possibilities available to them for a single inclusive admission charge.

Securing high levels of coverage at reasonable cost is the main objective of Beaulieu's marketing. To achieve this a local advertising agency is employed to handle all media space bookings and to design and produce advertisements and printed publicity material.

Colour leaflets provide information for visitors. Research indicates both the kind of information visitors require and also the most sensible places to distribute the leaflets. These leaflets are available at Tourist Information Centres and holiday accommodation sites, and are also distributed by direct mail and at travel trade fairs and exhibitions. Fairs and exhibitions offer attractions like Beaulieu the opportunity to encourage tour operators and travel agents to include visits to attractions in the tour programmes they offer.

Marketing staff at Beaulieu discussing promotional material.

Marketing opportunities sometimes arise through working with regional and national groups involved in tourism. The Regional Tourist Board and the local councils will generally have a vested interest in promoting the region and the attractions which lie within it. Members of national organisations, such as The Treasure Houses of England, or hotel marketing consortia, such as Best Western Hotels, can help to promote each other's interests. Beaulieu maintains links with other tourist facilities in the UK, especially through a consultancy and advisory service. Though an attraction might not wish to reveal sensitive information, such as its weekly takings, to a competitor, it might share market research for example, on the grounds that this could improve the performance of both attractions.

Your task

The previous information has been distributed to various managers at Beaulieu as the basis for a discussion of future marketing policy. In response, individual managers have highlighted the following issues and questions which could be considered in a planning meeting:

1   *The small percentage of the total number of visitors to Beaulieu made up of senior citizens:*
    ● possible reasons for this
    ● the type of promotional activity which might increase the percentage
    ● implications of a successful promotion to this market segment.

2   *Though Beaulieu is open all year round, 40% of visitors come during July and August*
    ● the type of promotional activity which might increase visitor numbers in, say, November or February
    ● the factors which would determine the budget set for such a promotional activity.

3   *Half the visitors to Beaulieu are adults with children:*
    ● the extent to which this should influence media chosen for advertising and design of publicity material.

4   *The average stay at Beaulieu is four hours:*
    ● should this be referred to in publicity materials?
    ● what are the implications of suggesting in publicity material that Beaulieu is worth a half day's or a full day's visit ?

5   *Many attractions have added entertainment facilities, such as fairgrounds*
    ● what would be the marketing implications if such an addition were considered at Beaulieu?

6   *Posters and advertising on the sides of buses are both recognised means of gaining publicity:*
    ● what advantages and disadvantages might each have as a means of publicising Beaulieu?
    ● how might you calculate their cost effectiveness?

7   *Beaulieu comprises a motor museum, a 13th century abbey, a historic country house and a maritime museum:*
    ● what common themes or threads can be identified to help to provide an overall picture of the various attractions?
    ● how would these be best used in marketing Beaulieu?

Debate these issues in small groups. You may wish to adopt the following roles:

- financial director
- personnel manager
- retail and catering manager
- marketing and PR manager
- Motor Museum manager
- Buckler's Hard manager.

3.7 Marketing national parks

Develops knowledge and understanding of the following element:

3.3 Investigate and evaluate marketing communications in leisure and tourism organisations

Supports development of the following core skills:

Communication 3.2 (Task 1)

Communication 3.2, 3.3 (Task 2)

The leisure and tourism industries place a heavy emphasis on successful marketing. Attractions and facilities compete with each other for visitors, but the product being sold is generally more complex than something people buy in a shop. While a souvenir may be judged in terms of its workmanship or aesthetic appeal, the visit during which it was bought will be judged in terms of the whole experience. This may include travel, accommodation, landscape, services and facilities. Planning the marketing of a souvenir is therefore always going to be simpler than the marketing of a destination.

Marketing a tourist destination becomes particularly difficult when there are a number of different attractions within a well defined area such as a national park. Many visitors will be touring the region rather than stopping in a single location. The first priority is usually to define the characteristics of the region which make it distinctive.

The Countryside Commission suggests that there are four ways in which individual enterprises can successfully improve their marketing:

- Obtaining accurate information about visitors is essential: knowing where they have come from, why they came, where they heard about the area and what they enjoyed or disliked about their visits can help individual leisure and tourism centres to plan ahead.
- Using this information to target markets lessens the chances of advertisements and direct mail failing to reach sympathetic audiences.
- Making sure that people enjoy their visits is a factor in good marketing. If people go away happy, they are more likely to make repeat visits and to be receptive to information about new developments in the region.
- Seeking professional advice, whether from a regional tourist board or a marketing company, may ultimately generate more visitors as a result of a specific campaign or promotion.

Yorkshire Dales National Park: Malham Cove.

Many leisure and tourism businesses, such as a bed and breakfast hotel or a boat hire company, are small operations. This means they do not have the funds for the more expensive kinds of promotion like glossy brochures or television advertising. However they can often benefit from group marketing. The National Farm Holiday Bureau for example coordinates the work of separate farm holiday groups in each of the national parks. Not only does this enable small enterprises to pool resources, but also to work jointly on creating common booking systems and developing tours and packages designed to appeal to specific markets.

One way of attracting and retaining visitors to areas like national parks is to provide them with a range of activities. These need to be locally available, clearly signed and well researched. They might also include instruction and demonstration in various skills and techniques. The Countryside Commission describes four ways of using these activities in marketing the area:

- send out information on these opportunities before arrival, or to past visitors. This might involve consulting with the national park authority in selecting particular events to promote
- put together and promote simple packages involving some of these activities, based on weekend breaks or longer stays, including off-season periods
- put together a walking or cycling package between a number of accommodation enterprises, with visitors' luggage transported between them
- work with other tourism enterprises, the national parks authority and other agencies to devise a comprehensive programme of walks, lectures, conservation work, etc., to give a varied and imaginative insight into the national park.

Your tasks

1 Identify a renovation or conservation scheme in need of voluntary labour. List the activities at the site which require labour and identify the skills which might be particularly useful.

75

Plan a programme of activities for visitors willing to spend part of their holiday in the region working on the scheme. The programme should indicate:

- the mix of work and leisure
- the accommodation to be used
- how the scheme is to be funded.

2 Design a leaflet, to be distributed in colleges and universities, which is intended to attract students to spend their summer vacations working on the project.

3.8 Presenting marketing plans for new products I

Develops knowledge and understanding of the following element:
3.4 Develop a marketing plan for a selected leisure and tourism product/service

Supports development of the following core skills:
Communication 3.1, 3.2 (Task 1)
Communication 3.2 (Task 2)

Introduction and background

A good marketing plan must be both feasible and based on well researched data. It needs to explain the background of the marketing idea and its objectives. It should indicate the research methods employed and the data used in forming a marketing strategy. The strategy itself is often described under four headings: product, place, price and promotion. No marketing plan would be complete without a budget statement itemising the plan's predicted costs.

The background to a marketing plan should explain how the idea for a new product or service came about and why it is appropriate at a particular time and in a particular area. The current popularity of a particular television series, for example, might be a reason for promoting themed short break holidays in the town or region where the series is set. The introduction to the plan could also discuss people's general spending habits in the region, suggesting why it is thought that there is a gap in the market. There should also be some general consideration both of the potential competition and of the likely stimuli for new products or services.

Marketing objectives may be either short term or long term. Short term objectives could involve piloting the new idea to see whether it needed modifying in any way. Certainly they would include identifying target markets and planning a marketing campaign. Short term objectives can also be very specific (such as finding out which three flavours of seaside rock are most popular) or they can be much broader, as in the case of a new Tourist Information Centre whose objective was to raise the profile of a specific destination. Long term objectives are also likely to contain broad statements about anticipated achievement. They could relate to quality of services or products or changes in public perceptions. Some objectives will have a commercial basis, for example they may refer to sales targets or increasing the frequency of visitors.

It is important in the marketing plan to provide an early assessment of the merits and possible weaknesses of the proposal. This is sometimes achieved by means of a SWOT analysis. This is a simple method of deciding whether a marketing idea is worth pursuing by listing its strengths, weaknesses, opportunities and threats. A company planning to market themed Sherlock Holmes weekends in London, for example, might produce a SWOT analysis which looked something like this:

Strengths
- Sherlock Holmes is an internationally known name.
- The subject has always been associated with London.
- No similar weekend break is currently available.
- Overseas visitors to London frequently inquire about Holmes.
- London offers a wide range of additional attractions.

Weaknesses
- Most places mentioned in the Holmes stories have lost their Victorian appearance.
- Tour parties in busy London streets have to be kept small.
- Attractions directly relating to Holmes are few in number.
- The market is limited to those with an interest in Sherlock Holmes.

Opportunities
- Sherlock Holmes stories have been recently serialised on television, showing both in the UK and overseas.
- Some historical aspects of Central London have not been fully exploited.

Threats
- The British weather!
- Perceived risks, especially by overseas visitors, of terrorist bomb attacks.
- The economic recession and unfavourable exchange rates.
- Competition from other tourist attractions.

Your tasks

1 Identify a single new product or service which you think might exploit a gap in the leisure and/or tourism markets. Devise a number of short term and long term objectives for marketing the product or service.
Discuss the factors which would control how successfully each of these objectives would be met.

2 Select one of the following proposals:
- an East Enders theme park in East London
- a Vietnamese Restaurant in a small town or village near where you live
- a dance studio in a mining village.

Write a SWOT analysis for the proposal you have chosen.

3.9 Presenting marketing plans for new products 2

Develops knowledge and understanding of the following element:

3.4   Develop a marketing plan for a selected leisure and tourism product/service

Supports development of the following core skills:

Application of number 3.2, 3.3 (Task 1)

Application of number 3.2, 3.3 (Task 2)

Application of number 3.2, 3.3 (Task 3)

Application of number 3.2, 3.3 (Task 4)

Application of number 3.2, 3.3 (Task 5)

Product, price, promotion, place

Products may be material objects such as goods sold in shops. In leisure and tourism, however, they are just as likely to be services, such as sports and entertainment ticket reservation services, the provision of restaurant meals, combinations of transport, facilities and accommodation or services creating excursions or tours.

If the new product was a themed break, the marketing plan would have to propose a detailed itinerary for potential customers. Details like transfers to and from airports or railway stations, timings of meals, roles to be played by guides and outside speakers, and any special clothing or equipment required would form part of the product description. The positive aspects of the product need to be emphasised if the company or a bank are to be persuaded to invest in it. Some aspects of the plan may require justification, for instance the decision to accommodate people in a particularly expensive hotel. In schemes where activities are involved, the plan may need to provide relevant detail about locations, safety, transport, special clothing and equipment and any extra costs.

However good the product, the marketing will not be effective if the price is unrealistic. Any scheme will have to cover all the *fixed* costs before a profit can be made. In the case of a themed break the fixed costs would include some transport costs like coach hire, and some fixed service costs, such as fees for guides and speakers. The *variable* costs would include accommodation and meals. These would vary according to the number of people actually taking the break. The money received from each person will exceed the average cost of the product or service and that difference will represent the profit to be made. The plan has to calculate both the amount of profit needed to make the proposal worthwhile and viable, while at the same time estimating what potential purchasers will regard as value for money.

Promotion is the part of the marketing plan intended to increase demand for the product. The type of promotion featured will depend largely on the target market, though cost will also be a factor. There would be more point in advertising a new cricketing holiday to Corfu in Cricket Monthly than in The Angling Times. Planning a new leisure centre in Penzance might involve direct mail as a means of promotion, but the letters would only be sent to those within reasonable travelling distance of the proposed development. Advertising in the national press or on television may have the advantage of reaching a very wide audience, but it may also be far more costly than the likely revenue from the scheme could justify. The majority of readers or viewers may in any case fall outside the market segments likely to be interested in the product.

In order to reach defined target markets, the plan must show how and where promotional materials are to be distributed. Brochures about new tourist attractions, for example, might be distributed from tourist information centres, travel agents, public libraries and hotels in the same region. They could, however, also be distributed outside the region through places like railway stations and at travel trade exhibitions and fairs. Tour operators might be persuaded to include the brochure in information packs sent out to customers booking tours in the region.

Your tasks

Look at the figures in the table below which give the fixed and variable costs of a proposed weekend holiday package based on a Sherlock Holmes theme. The package costs are calculated on the basis of thirty people taking part.

Fixed and variable costs must be covered before any profit can be made. In this instance, the package just about breaks even with the thirteenth guest. With the chosen price the **contribution margin** of £93.83 will be made on a full tour.

Now answer the following questions.

1 How much profit will be made on the full tour?

2 What will be the total variable costs for 30 people if discounts for groups are discontinued?

3 There are ten fully refunded cancellations, but the discounts shown are still applicable to the variable costs for the remainder of the party. At the price of £266.63 per person, what will the total revenue be?

4 If it is considered that average revenue per person cannot be increased, how many additional people would need to book beyond the first 30 to make a second tour party worthwhile? Fixed costs for the whole package double for any group size between 31 and 60.

5 No figures for office and administration overheads have been included in this example. Would these items be included as fixed or variable costs, and why?

Fixed costs	All figures in £
Apix Coaches Ltd. 1 x whole day hire @ 175 = 175 2 x half day hire @ 90 = 180	355.00
London carriages Ltd. 6 x @ 50 per hour for 5 persons	300.00
Livetts Launches Cost for boat hire	400.00
Frashards Ltd. Waitress service for boat dinner	35.00
Tour guides and speakers 5 x @ 25 per hour	125.00
Total fixed costs	1215.00

(Continued)

Variable costs	All figures in £

Sherlock Holmes Hotel
14 x @125 for double/twin rooms
2 x @105 for single rooms

2 nights accommodation = 3920 (10% discount for groups)	3528.00

Frashards Ltd

30 x @10.75 per person for buffet dinner	322.50

Sherlock Holmes Pub

30 x @8 per person for pub lunch = 240 (10% discount for groups)	216.00

Golden Tours

30 x @22 per person for show and supper	660.00

Simpsons in The Strand

30 x @12.50 per person for lunch = 375 (10% discount for groups)	337.50

Sherlock Holmes Hotel

30 x @4 per person for afternoon tea	120.00

Total variable costs	5184.00
Total costs: fixed costs	1215.00
variable costs	5184.00
	6399.00
Total cost per person	213.30
Average revenue per person	
(20% profit)	266.63
Total revenue	7998.75

3.10 Advertising

Develops knowledge and understanding of the following element:
3.4   Develop a marketing plan for a selected leisure and tourism product/service

Supports development of the following core skills:
Application of number 3.2; Communication 3.4 (Task 1)
Application of number 3.2; Communication 3.4 (Task 2)
Communication 3.2, 3.3 (Task 3)

The main function of advertising is to make people more aware of the products or services being offered. The hope of the advertisers is that this will affect consumer choice. For example, some people will choose holiday destinations because they have featured in advertising campaigns. Others may already have decided where to go but will choose a Thomsons holiday rather than a Have-Fun-in-the-Sun Limited holiday because they are aware of the former company but have never heard of the latter.

Advertising has been defined as 'any paid form of non-personal presentation and promotion of ideas, products or services by an identified sponsor'. In other words it is always a commercial transaction directed by whoever is paying for it at the general public. It is used to explain what products and services are available and how these can be used. Above all, advertising aims to persuade potential buyers that a particular product or service is superior to any similar ones. Advertisers hope that the end result will be an increase in sales, particularly in the short term. A better public knowledge of the company and its products or services may enable it to increase its share of existing markets and perhaps develop new ones.

Holiday advertising in a national newspaper.

A common system of analysing advertisements is known by the acronym AIDA: attention, interest, desire and action. This describes the process by which a good advertisement is expected to have its impact. An advertisement which fails to capture attention at the outset is unlikely to be effective. Written advertisements may use witty headlines, large print or cartoon drawings to attract attention. Television advertising is more likely to rely on a combination of striking images and distinctive soundtracks.

The message of the advertisement can only be put across fully if interest is sustained throughout. A holiday brochure may offer entrance into a prize draw for readers who extract answers from the text. A number of recent television advertisements have introduced on-going narratives based around the featured product in which the watchers are really being invited to speculate about what will happen to the relationships between the characters.

If the advertisement holds the interest but does not make the audience want to buy the service or product, the company has gained no return for its investment. Advertising is constantly seeking to latch on to common consumer motivation. Leisure advertising often focuses on the benefits of a healthy life-style. Holiday advertising may stress the need for rest and relaxation, or it may try to make people think of the aspects of their daily routine from which they would like to escape.

Consumers may of course be persuaded that they want a holiday or a healthier life-style, but this does not necessarily mean that they will go out out and spend money on them. From an advertiser's point of view the good advertisement must lead directly to actual sales. Where products are fairly similar, for example two package holidays to the same destination using similar standard accommodation, advertisers may use pricing policies as a means of persuading customers to buy. Discounts may be an inducement because people believe they are saving money. Knowing the price of something before buying it may also encourage customers, particularly those on a limited budget.

Your tasks

Avernice Tripp Ltd, a small travel agency in Easthampton specialising in holidays to France, wishes to boost its sales in the period immediately after Christmas. The agency is considering advertising as a means of achieving this. Preliminary research has revealed the following:

Local Press
The weekly Easthampton Gazette has a circulation of 25 000 and charges £225 for each quarter-page advertisement.

Local Radio
Listen East, the local radio station, claims it can be received in 50 000 homes, though local research suggests only 20 per cent listen regularly. A two-minute advertising slot at a favourable time costs £400.

Regional Television
ETV, the regional independent channel, gives access to 120 000 homes, though only a third of these are in Easthampton itself. A 30-second advertisement would cost £750, but would cost £4 000 to make.

Direct Mail
A local direct mail company, using information built up from credit records, will send out promotional letters designed and printed by the advertisers at £350 per 1000. Writing and printing the promotional material would add a further £1250 to the cost.

1   Given that Avernice Tripp Ltd makes an average profit of £40 on each holiday sold, how much extra business do you think they would need to generate to make each of the four listed methods of advertising worthwhile?

2   What do you think would be the benefits and potential risks of each of these four methods of advertising?

   Which single medium do you think would most effectively meet the company's needs? What reasons can you give to support this view?

3   Avernice Tripp Limited is particularly concerned that they are losing customers to a small specialist tour operator in the town, Vacances Jacques. This company specialises in self-catering accommodation and has been undercutting Avernice Tripp's prices for similar holidays.

   Present a plan for a promotion specifically aimed at enabling Tripps to ward off this competition.

Unit 4 Finance in the leisure and tourism industries

4.1 Raising finance for projects

Develops knowledge and understanding of the following element:
4.1   Investigate the financial performance of leisure and tourism organisations

Supports development of the following core skills:
Communication 3.4 (Task 1)
Application of number 3.1; Communication 3.2; Information Technology 3.1, 3.3 (Task 2)

Anyone thinking of starting up a caravan park, converting a house into holiday apartments or developing any other leisure or tourism scheme must first of all make sure that they have sufficient finance. They must also be sure that there is enough demand for the product or service to:
- pay the costs of this finance
- provide them with an adequate income.

Banks will lend money for projects, but only if they are satisfied that the proposition is viable. The major banks advise potential borrowers to prepare a business plan. The plan should cover a number of important areas:
- the scheme's objectives
- its potential market
- the nature of the product or service being offered
- the intended pricing policy
- the supplies, premises and equipment needed
- any extra personnel to be employed
- the expertise and experience of the proposer of the project
- the marketing plans
- the book-keeping and recording system to be used.

Perhaps the most difficult part of the business plan is estimating accurately the level of sales which can be achieved. A hotel planning an extension will have to calculate what rate of room occupancy it can reasonably expect to achieve and what it would require in order to break even. **Cash flow** is also important: a travel agent specialising in business travel may find itself waiting for accounts to be settled by its customers at the end of a quarterly period and not having sufficient cash to pay its weekly and monthly bills.

There is plenty of professional advice available to people planning new projects. In addition to the banks themselves, local trade associations, Regional Tourist Boards, and national organisations like the Rural Development Commission may be able to offer guidance and opinions about the likely **viability** of the proposal. In some regions there may be grants available for developments which meet specified criteria. These are more common in areas of declining industry, in those facing depopulation and in inner city areas needing **regeneration.**

Before banks will agree to lend money, they need to be sure that businesses can cope with unexpected setbacks. If the cost of building extra hotel rooms proves greater than expected, they may wish to know whether the hotel owner would raise prices (and risk attracting fewer guests), or whether they would reduce costs by dismissing staff (and risk a lower level of service). Since hotels often depend on repeat business, it would be counter-productive to cut the costs of a new development if facilities or services then appeared to the guests to be inferior.

Most banks lending large sums for business projects will ask for some kind of **security.** The value of the security will need to be higher than the amount lent, with a safety margin between the two sums so that both parties have some degree of protection if things go wrong. Many borrowers will offer **freehold** land or property as security against the loan, others will **remortgage** property to raise cash to invest in a business scheme. As hotel owners have found recently, remortgaging property can harm a business if property values fall sharply and the renegotiated mortgage stands at a higher value than the **market value** of the property. Machinery or equipment is rarely accepted as security.

Banks will probably expect business borrowers to invest an amount from their own funds to match the sum the bank is lending them. This is to show that the borrower is committed to making a success of the project, as well as limiting the extent of the bank's loss if the scheme fails. Most lenders will also insist on the borrower taking out an insurance policy, so that the loan is repaid if the borrower dies or is unable to work because of an accident or ill health.

The structure of loan repayments may vary considerably too.
- The interest to be repaid may be at a fixed rate, or may vary according to changes in the bank's **base rate.**
- Special terms may be available for business starters which postpone all repayments for an agreed period while the business is getting established.

A government Loan Guarantee Scheme will in some circumstances guarantee most of a loan in return for a **premium payment** of 2.5 per cent of the guaranteed amount.

Your tasks

1 Write definitions of the following words or phrases used in the passage above: viable, break even, cash flow, security, remortgage, base rate, premium payment.

2 You decide to set up a new business making and selling small souvenirs of the region in which you live.

Draw up the first draft of a business plan which will enable you to do the following things:
- decide whether the business will work
- identify the income and expenditure involved
- monitor the progress of the business
- provide your bank with sufficient background for them to judge whether and how they might help you.

4.2 Evaluating the financial performance of a guest house

Develops knowledge and understanding of the following element:

4.1 Investigate the financial performance of leisure and tourism organisations

Supports development of the following core skills:

Application of number 3.2, 3.3 (Task 1)

Application of number 3.3; Communication 3.4 (Task 2)

'Stumbleside' is a small guest house in the Lake District. Established in their stone-built former family home by Mr and Mrs Reg Guest in the 1930s, it is now run by their son, Phil, and his wife, Sue.

Running a small business like this is not just a matter of sitting and waiting for people to arrive in the summer holidays. There are all year round costs involved in running a guest house and the owners' aim must be to keep it as full as possible for as long as possible. The Lake District attracts people during all holidays, including Easter, Whit, Christmas and school half terms. It is also a popular destination with people looking for weekend or mid-week short breaks.

In previous years Stumbleside has achieved an occupancy rate of approximately 60 per cent. As a business it does currently make a net profit, even when the owners draw personal wages of £5000. This sum is agreed with the Inland Revenue as being a reasonable wage to draw, being roughly what it would cost to employ someone else to do the work involved. The owners will have to pay some tax on any profit they make.

Cashflow figures play an important role in running any business. Even in a profitable business it may prove impossible to pay debts at particular times of year if the movement of cash through the business is not properly managed. If all creditors decide to call in the money owed to them at the same time a company can become insolvent, despite the expectation that it would have made a profit over the whole year. For many businesses this means they have to borrow money and repay it when their revenue is at its peak. Cashflow calculations enable a business to predict the flow of money over time and to plan strategies to cope with periods showing a deficit.

The owners of Stumbleside have a number of possible ways of improving cash flow. They can reinvest their profits into the business. They could seek to defer or spread their payments more evenly. The latter can be done by using budget bank accounts to pay some bills in instalments. They could seek higher deposits or earlier payments from their customers or tighten up on their procedures for extracting some sort of compensatory payment from customers who make late cancellations.

Your tasks

Study the business summary and the cashflow summary on the following pages and then answer the questions which follow on page 88.

Stumbleside Guest House: summary of current business

1. **Location**	The Lake District	
2. **Season**	February–December plus Christmas/New Year period. Closed 7 January–14 February approx.	
3. **Rooms**	5 x double occupancy, 2 x single occupancy, 1 x family occupancy (four maximum including two children up to 16 years of age)	

4. **Rates per night**   (Bed & breakfast)

	Adults	**Children** (one free if sharing)	**Single supplement**
	(£)	(%)	(£)
Feb–Mar (46 nights)	12	50	1
April–May (61 nights)	14	50	1
June–Sept (122 nights)	15	50	2
Oct–Nov (61 nights)	12	50	1
1 Dec–21 Dec (21 nights)	11	50	nil
21 Dec–7 Jan (18 nights)	15	50	2

The 47-week opening period (329 nights) aims at 60 per cent occupancy at adult rates, disregarding child reductions and room supplements. In other words 14 adult beds per night represents 100 per cent occupancy.

5. **Maximum possible revenue**

```
 46  x £12 x 14 =   £7728
 61  x £14 x 14 = £11 956
122  x £15 x 14 = £25 620
 61  x £12 x 14 = £10 248
 21  x £11 x 14 =   £3234
 18  x £15 x 14 =   £3780
```

Total   = £62 566

6. **Anticipated revenue**

60% x £62 566 = £37 500

7. **Actual revenue**

Sales	B & B room occupancy	36 784			
	Packed lunches	494			
		37 278			**37 278**
Less: Cost of sales	Bedding	941			
	Food ingredients/grocery	2100			
		3041		**3041**	
	Overheads				
	Mortgage	4980			
	Light/heat/water	948			
	Rates (Unified Business)	3500			
	Repairs and maintenance	2000			
	Drawings (owners' salaries)	5000			
	Other salaries/wages	4300			
	Insurance	752			
	Telephone	842			
	Stationery	759			
	Advertising	650			
	Postages	700			
	Sundry items	451			
		24 882			
			24 882		
			27 923		**27 923**
Net profit					**9355**

Finance in the leisure and tourism industries

Stumbleside Guest House: summary of current business

Item	F	M	A	M	J	J	A	S	O	N	D	J	Notes
Revenue													
B&B	1274	3362	3196	3958	3132	3684	4188	4368	4184	1229	3141	1068	(36784)
Other	24	42	38	45	44	52	60	64	52	28	35	10	(494) Fewer lunches in bad weather
Total income	**1298**	**3404**	**3234**	**4003**	**3176**	**3736**	**4248**	**4432**	**4236**	**1257**	**3176**	**1078**	**(37278)**
Costs													
Food	84	165	142	178	212	172	424[1]	211	192	68	102	150	(2100) [1]Bulk purchase
Bedding	424	–	–	–	317	–	–	200	–	–	–	–	(941)
Mortgage	415	415	415	415	415	415	415	415	415	415	415	415	(4980)
Light/heat/water	82	64	74	80	78	82	68	84	94	90	88	64	(948) Varies with demands for hot water, heat, etc.
Rates (Unified business)	–	–	1750	–	–	–	–	1750	–	–	–	–	(3500) Twice p.a.
Repairs/maintenance	984[2]	–	–	250	42	150	40	–	92	400[3]	–	42	(2000) [2]Decoration while closed [3]Burst pipe
Drawings	–	1250	–	–	1250	–	–	1250	–	–	1250	–	(5000) Quarterly for proprietor
Salaries/wages	100	120	200	400	550	560	600	610	421	329	300	110	(4300) Spouse plus casual staff employed
Insurance	–	548[4]	–	–	–	204[5]	–	–	–	–	–	–	(752) 2 × Annual premiums; [4]Public liability; [5]Buildings
Telephone	226	–	–	236	–	–	192	–	–	188	–	–	(842) Quarterly
Stationery	32	30	40	28	22	25	28	20	18	–	410	106	(759)
Advertising	254	–	–	–	–	–	–	–	–	–	–	396	(650) Seasonal items to attract customers
Postage	174	82	50	48	56	12	14	40	32	30	34	128	(700)
Sundries	10	18	–	121	39	80	74	22	37	0	0	32	(451)
Total costs	**2785**	**2692**	**2671**	**1756**	**2981**	**1700**	**1855**	**4602**	**1301**	**1529**	**2608**	**1443**	**(27 923)**
Surplus/deficit	−1487	+712	+563	+2247	+195	+2036	+2393	−170	+2935	−272	+568	−365	
Funds available at:													
a) the start of month	2000	513	1225	1788	4035	4230	6266	8659	8489	11 424	11 152	11 720	(including £20000 b/f Feb 92)
b) the end of month	513	1225	1788	4035	4230	6266	8659	8489	11 424	11 152	11 720	11 355	

1 a) Identify which expenses are unavoidable in the early months of the calendar year, even though income is low, and explain why this is so.

b) Which was the guest house's best month for sales and why did it not make a profit in that month?

c) What would happen to September's deficit figures if occupancy was increased by 10 per cent, taking into account that additional food, costing £40, would have to be bought in?

d) Do you see any opportunity for other sales to boost total income, in addition to packed lunches?

e) What reasons can you suggest for the fact that May revenue exceeds that of June, even though room rates charged in June are higher?

f) What factors should the owners take into account in deciding the relative room rates fixed for May and June?

g) What arguments can you think of for and against the owners keeping the guest house open in November and early December?

h) Why might it be a good idea for the owners to use budget bank accounts as a means of settling some of their expenditure?

i) If the Guests were attempting to buy the hotel now, as opposed to fifteen years ago when they bought it from the senior Guests, they would need a larger mortgage, approximately doubling their monthly repayments. Indicate the consequences of this for the monthly profitability of the business.

j) Can you think of ways in which the Guests might boost occupancy or provide added value which would enable them to increase prices?

k) The average price of an 8-bedroomed house in the Lake District similar to Stumbleside is £60 000. Explain why you would or would not be willing to pay £80 000 for the 'Stumbleside' guest house business.

2 Read the article below taken from 'The Lake District Echo' published on 7 February 1993:

Hotels and guesthouses suffered in 1992

'One of the Lake District's major employment sectors is suffering badly in the present economic climate.

A good May last year, with guesthouses in particular about 60 per cent full, was followed by a poor June with less than 50 per cent average bed occupancy.

The only boom month was September with popular addresses recording up to 90% figures in the excellent Indian summer which attracted older visitors to The Lakes after the end of the school holidays. This helped offset the disastrously wet June, July and August, when often three beds in four went unsold each night and a 50 per cent occupancy rate was regarded as a success.

October and November were better than some expected with up to 55% figures in some businesses, but the very miserable Christmas weather left our area almost empty. "You were doing better than many if 10 per cent of beds went daily," said Mo Smart on behalf of the local hospitality association.

Now there is a threat hanging over the new season. Guests are preferring establishments offering evening meals. "Owners will have to respond even though the requirement to provide food around 7–8 p.m. often hardly covers the costs," said a representative of the Regional Tourist Board.'

Use the article and the data you have about Stumbleside to evaluate the performance of the business over the year.

4.3 Evaluating the business performance of a leisure park

Develops knowledge and understanding of the following element:
4.1 Investigate the financial performance of leisure and tourism organisations

Supports development of the following core skills:
Application of number 3.3; Communication 3.1 (Task 1)
Application of number 3.3; Communication 3.1 (Task 2)

Leisure parks, like most other businesses, exist to make a profit. As a result the measurement of their success must include the setting of financial targets which are likely to be divided into two main categories: the return on the capital invested, and the trading margin.

A successful leisure park will certainly require investment. The cost of purchasing a new ride, for example, can be in excess of £10 million. If the park is starting from scratch, as in the case of EuroDisney, the amount of new investment will be higher than that needed in an established park. Funds will be needed for construction, legal and architects' fees, landscaping, and salaries before any income has been generated. An older park is likely to have a broader capital base. This means more of the money it needs to operate, including investment in new development, is likely to come from its own assets which have been derived from previous years' profits or from its own successful investments.

Gardens at Alton Towers.

Pearson plc, the owners of Alton Towers, invested some £60 million in the Park in 1990. If they had put that sum into a building society in that year, they might have received 15 per cent interest as a return on their investment. Investing the money in a leisure park is regarded as carrying a higher risk and so investors require a higher return, in this case possibly in excess of 25 per cent. In other words Pearsons might have set a financial objective for Alton Towers for 1990, aiming for a return of £15 million.

Regardless of the level of investment, a leisure park will measure its trading profitability. This is essentially a matter of subtracting costs from sales. The trading margin must be sufficient to generate a return on the capital investment. In other words, as for any other business, it is not enough for a leisure park company simply to make a trading profit.

At Alton Towers management accounts are published annually, though the data for these is internally circulated on a quarterly basis. The accounts take the form of a profit and loss account, which gives a financial measure of performance over a period of time. Such accounts can be accompanied by a commentary offering views about trends identified within them, for example high costs in a particular area might be the result of possible over-staffing.

The advantage of quarterly reviews of figures is that they avoid the difficulty of judging on a month by month basis, where fluctuations can be misleading. Quarterly figures also enable comparisons to be made between years on a seasonal basis. If the figures revealed that business performance was not as good as had been expected, a number of immediate responses might be possible. It might be possible to reduce overheads in some way. Discount offers or special deals might be used to try and attract more visitors. It might be possible to offer added value without a very high investment, for example by offering a free guide book or by offering free admission to a child accompanied by a paying adult.

Alton Towers.   The Alton Towers accounts will include forecasts of future income, derived from

admission charges and from secondary sales through food and retail outlets. Income is dependent on the volume of visitors and their individual spend. Since all leisure parks have a finite capacity, the upper limits of income are fixed as long as the admission price remains the same. Leisure park customers are unlikely to respond positively to price increases unless they feel some additional value has been provided. This means that profit growth is dependent on capital investment, since that is the best way of improving the product and thus allowing acceptable price increases and a rise in income.

Your tasks

The two pie charts below represent the percentage of total expenditure in a medium-sized leisure park devoted to different categories in the years 1991 and 1992.

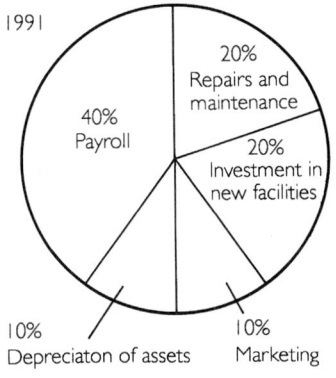 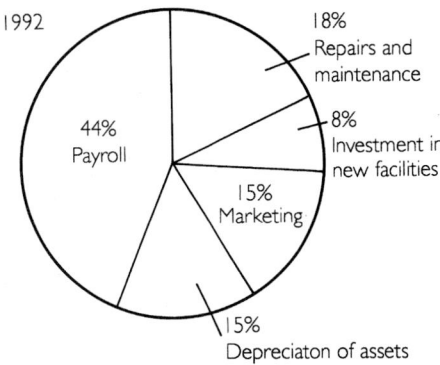

1 Discuss what evidence you can see to suggest that the following statements are either probably true, possibly true, unlikely, or impossible to determine:

   a) More staff were employed in 1991 than 1992.

   b) An evaluation of 1990's business performance suggested some added value was needed.

   c) Television advertising was first tried in 1992.

   d) Older equipment has proved more costly to maintain over this two-year period.

   e) Investing in new facilities has long term financial implications.

2 The leisure park management consider that 1992 was a success and they predict that the number of visitors will continue to increase in 1993.

   Assuming that this proves to be the case, discuss the various possible implications of the two following expenditure forecasts for 1993.

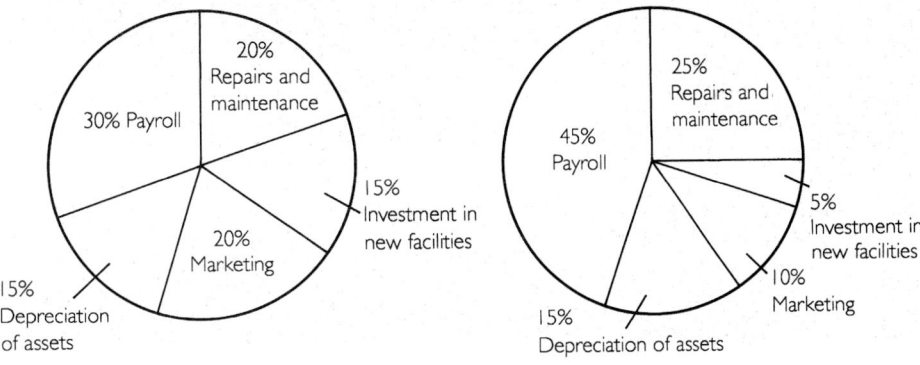

4.4 The National Trust: sources of funding

Develops knowledge and understanding of the following element:

4.2 Examine financial accounts in leisure and tourism organisations

Supports development of the following core skills:

Communication 3.4 (Task 1)

Communication 3.1 (Task 2)

Tourists who are fond of the countryside, and in particular of country houses, owe much to the National Trust. The Trust manages and conserves much important landscape and many historic properties. Keeping up this work demands extensive funds. These are drawn from a variety of sources. The following extract, adapted from the National Trust's Annual Report of 1991, describes how the organisation gained and managed its financial resources:

National Trust land at Ravenscar, North Yorkshire.

During 1991 the Chancellor of the Exchequer raised the rate of VAT by 2½ per cent which resulted in a loss to the Trust of some £800 000. Income from **deeds of covenant** on members' subscriptions was affected by a change in the Inland Revenue's rules which now requires covenants to last for a minimum of four years. This made it difficult to retain the proportion of members willing to sign them.

Despite these problems the Trust succeeded in increasing its profits through the trading activities of National Trust Enterprises Limited. Though there was a decline in the number of paying visitors and in agricultural rents, income from **legacies** reached a record level. Membership grew by almost 6 per cent during the year and non-agricultural rents increased by 7 per cent. The huge growth in membership over the last 25 years makes it unlikely that it will increase further. This has also resulted in a reduction of paying visitors to individual properties, since membership of the Trust gives free entry to these.

National Trust Enterprises Limited produced a **turnover** of more than £30 million, mainly through its retailing, catering and holiday cottage activities. However, such enterprises require new investment each year. Catering outlets may need funds to ensure that they comply with the provisions of the new Food Safety Act. Some of the Trust's shops were refitted and a number of new ones were opened. Approximately 200 products were introduced, including new toiletries, conserves, home fragrances and pottery. The company offered a number of specialist holidays within the United Kingdom, as well as cruises to Norway and the Rhine.

The Trust received funding from a number of companies during 1991. British Gas became their largest sponsor to date by providing £500 000 over five years to support the work of the Trust's wardens. Barclays Bank are providing £350 000 over six years to support the Young National Trust Theatre. Other sponsors supported events such as concerts or firework displays at individual National Trust properties.

Other important sources of income include **charitable trusts** which increasingly recognise the direct social impact of many of the Trust's projects, particularly those which create employment, help to maintain communities, or make special provision for young people or those with disabilities. Appeals associated with particular regions, such as the Snowdonia Appeal, did well during the year, and new appeals for work in the Yorkshire Moors and Dales and on the South Downs were launched in the autumn. Regional projects also benefited from contributions from the European Regional Development Fund.

The extensive programme of **capital works** carried out by the Trust is very dependent on **bequests.** These are normally used in the year after receipt either for major restoration projects at existing properties or to buy and endow new properties. £23.5 million came to the Trust in 1991 as a result of legacies. Some of these specified how and where the money was to be used, but the remainder will largely be spent on the 1992 Capital Programme which includes activities such as:

- building restoration
- farm buildings
- landscape conservation
- visitors and access
- drains and sewers
- fire and security.

In terms of future needs, the Trust has identified £125 million worth of capital works which need to be completed on its properties in the next five years. As a high proportion of the National Trust's funds is committed to specific purposes, especially the **endowment** of properties, it will have to go on increasing its income if it is to complete the identified capital works, improve its standard of property management, and rescue important new properties.

1 Answer the following questions, some of which may require research:

   a) What is VAT? When is there no requirement to pay VAT?

   b) What is a deed of covenant? Why might the Inland Revenue's change of rules make National Trust members less willing to sign these?

   c) What reasons might you suggest to explain the National Trust's thirteen-fold increase in membership over the last 25 years?

   d) What sort of products can be bought in National Trust shops? What reasons can you give to explain why the Trust concentrates on this particular range of products?

   e) What do you think the companies who sponsor various aspects of the National Trust's work get in return for their investment?

   f) What does endow mean? What specific activities might the National Trust have to undertake in order to endow a new property?

2 List as many arguments as you can think of for and against the following points of view:

   a) 'The name, National Trust, doesn't give a clear enough message to the public about what the organisation actually does.'

   b) 'The National Trust should be wholly funded by central government.'

   c) 'The principles of profit-making and the principles of conservation are essentially incompatible.'

   d) 'Instead of spending money restoring historic houses, more funds should be directed towards building much-needed new houses.'

   With a partner, discuss the strength and weakness of the arguments you have listed.

4.5 Financing a tourism business – Dales Cottage Holidays

Develops knowledge and understanding of the following element:
4.2   Examine financial accounts in leisure and tourism organisations

Supports development of the following core skills:
Application of number 3.1; Communication 3.4; Information Technology 3.1, 3.2, 3.3 (Task 1)
Communication 3.1, 3.4 (Task 2)
Application of number 3.2, 3.3 (Task 3)

Dales Cottage Holidays is a business based in a North Yorkshire market town. It was started in the 1980s, initially financed by the profits from a service business based in the south of England. The first investment involved the purchase of a property right in the centre of the town. The location of the building was very important in business terms. Its central position, in the high street, made it very visible to visitors and passers-by.

Any small business will need some capital in its first year of operation. Developers of a country cottage operation need enough funds to see them through the year while the business gets under way. Initial costs will include premises, office equipment and stationery. Rent, council taxes, insurance, heat, lighting and leasing agreements for equipment will be expenses which will have to be met as the business develops.

Funds may come from a variety of sources. The most common is to seek a bank loan. This will generally only be granted if the applicants can offer some kind of security, such as property, against the loan. The bank may also expect the applicants to invest an amount of their own equivalent to the loan they are seeking. They will also have to prepare a detailed business plan, showing their objectives, their potential market, their pricing policy, their marketing intentions, and the methods of accounting and record keeping they intend to keep.

Sometimes funds are available from other sources. For example, Dales Cottage Holidays has benefited from a scheme providing rapid printouts of which cottages and bed and breakfast facilities are available in towns and villages within a 40-mile radius of its base. Daily lists can be generated, showing what sized accommodation is still free. Separate lists can indicate the vacancies in each town or village. The money to develop this scheme was obtained from the Rural Development Commission and from European Community funds intended to help the economic development of rural areas.

Dales Cottage Holidays manages 100 properties, the great majority of which are privately owned. The company manages the process of advertising the properties and renting them out on behalf of the owners. In return for this service, Dales Cottage Holidays receives 25 per cent of whatever holidaymakers pay to rent the cottages.

Like all businesses, Dales Cottage Holidays has to ensure that its income is sufficient to cover all its expenses, and leave its owners sufficient profit to make their efforts and the risk of investing their own money worth while. Income is clearly not going to be equal throughout the year. Even for the most desirable cottages, the rental season lasts between 40 and 46 weeks. The average number of bookings per cottage is 31. The rents themselves vary, depending on the time of year. The table on page 96 indicates the seasonal variation in weekly rents for three of the cottages available.

Sustaining as high an income as possible depends on being available to take bookings at the times potential customers find it convenient to make contact. Ninety per cent of all bookings taken are made over the telephone and phone lines are staffed from 9 a.m. until 7 p.m. seven days a week. This has implications for the costs of running the business. Clearly, telephone charges will be high, although British Telecom provides discounts for frequent users. Operating the phone lines 70 hours a week also means employment costs rise. Two people can be employed to work 35 hours each, but other staff will have to be available to cover holidays and sick leave. In a small business the owners will generally have to be able and willing to carry out any of the duties required in running the operation. As it grows its staff costs will rise, though in tourism the use of part-time staff helps to keep them within the budget available.

Income also depends on establishing the right price structure for the various cottage owners. Too high a price will put a property out of reach of many potential customers. Too low a price will mean the loss of potential profit. Before a price for each property can be

95

PEAK SEASON (9 weeks)	27 May–3 June 22 July–2 September 20 December–3 January	Ashlyns £360 Hazeley Hall £500 Fellside Cottage £275
HIGH SEASON (4 weeks)	8–22 July 2–9 September 21–28 October	Ashlyns £300 Hazeley Hall £440 Fellside Cottage £240
MID SEASON (8 weeks)	8–22 April 10 June–8 July 9–23 September	Ashlyns £250 Hazeley Hall £385 Fellside Cottage £215
LOW SEASON (3 weeks)	20–27 May 3–10 June 23–30 September	Ashlyns £210 Hazeley Hall £340 Fellside Cottage £190
WINTER SEASON (20 weeks)	January–1 April 28 October–20 December	Ashlyns £155 Hazeley Hall £250 Fellside Cottage £140
AUTUMN SAVERS	30 September–21 October	Ashlyns £185 Hazeley Hall £300 Fellside Cottage £170
SPRING SAVERS	1–8 April 22 April–20 May	Ashlyns £170 Hazeley Hall £275 Fellside Cottage £155

established, the owners have to decide what their prime purpose in renting out their cottage is. The average cost of a cottage in the Dales, based on 1995 prices, is about £60 000. Owners might receive a net return of about £4000 to £5000 a year. They will then have to pay business rates on the property, and various service and rental charges for power, water and telephone supply. Assuming that they have not bought the cottage on a mortgage, renting a cottage out will enable owners to cover all the standing (overhead) costs, including heating, around the year and make a profit as well. This profit is taxed by the Inland Revenue as a special dispensation under Schedule D, that is as a business, so all repairs and replacements, including furniture, and any mortgage interest to be paid, can be set against tax. This is particularly valuable to owners who pay higher rates of income tax. Since many of the cottages are either second homes or integral parts of family farms, the owners may wish to set a reasonable rent because their main purpose is to keep the property occupied, and therefore more secure and better looked after than if it was left empty. They will also be able to reduce their property overhead costs. Other owners may wish to maximise the amount they receive from rents, by setting them as high as the market will pay.

The main factors involved in setting a price for a cottage are its location, the views which can be seen from its windows and garden, the standard of the accommodation itself and whether parking spaces are available on the site. Holidaymakers generally expect the facilities to match those they have at home. This means that central heating and a refrigerator are absolute essentials, while most people will also want television and a washing machine. Decisions have to be taken about what to include in the price. Some cottages may include linen, but the laundry costs associated with this are between £10 and £12 a week. Heating is generally included in the price but is most costly – about £35 a week in

February – when the rents are lowest. In other words, over the whole year's business it is clear that summer bookings to some extent subsidise winter ones.

The attractive landscape of North Yorkshire makes it the kind of destination to which people grow attached. The more tenants Dales Cottage Holidays can persuade to return, the less they will have to spend on advertising to attract new customers. In fact 40 per cent of the company's business is made up of returning tenants. Nevertheless, marketing activities cost the company almost £30 000 a year. The costs of placing advertisements in different places have to be weighed up against the likely amount of new business they will generate. The business is sufficiently large to advertise in the national press and on teletext. Local newspapers and periodicals such as *The Dalesman* and *Woman's Own* are also used. The company advertises in most of the guides and brochures featuring North Yorkshire as a holiday destination. This includes annual guides to the region, Tourist Board guides and short breaks brochures. The policy of Dales Cottage Holidays is to spread the net wide, placing small adverts in the widest range of different publications.

A major cost for many holiday companies is brochure production. These are often expensively produced, with many coloured illustrations intended to impress on readers the attractions of the region and the accommodation being advertised. Dales Cottage Holidays has devised a less expensive system of brochure production which has the extra benefit of being extremely flexible. Each property is featured on a separate sheet, containing information about its location and facilities, and a line drawing showing the building's exterior. When telephone bookings are taken the computerised booking system will generate an individual letter listing all the properties which match the requirements of the customer. They can then be sent information about these properties, without having to study the full list, including those cottages which would not be suitable. The speed and efficiency of computer-generated information is essential to the success of the business.

All businesses have to ensure that they avoid problems with cash flow. There will generally be costs throughout the year, but cash may be received at irregular intervals. It is important, therefore, to ensure that payment from customers is received as early as possible so that the company has enough money in the bank to pay bills and wages. Dales Cottage Holidays requires customers to pay a 50 per cent deposit on booking a one-week stay and a 25 per cent deposit for each two-week booking. The balance is either paid two weeks before the holiday commences or is paid direct to the owners on arrival.

Your tasks

The owner of *The Crooked Mile* has approached Dales Cottage Holidays with a view to renting out her cottage for a year, commencing in January 1996.

A description, shown on page 98 is prepared, ready for entry into the company's new brochure.

The owner of the cottage regards it as a sound investment. She paid £25 000 for it in 1982, saw its value rise to an estimated £90 000 in 1988 and estimates its market value at about £69 500 now. However, she does not feel it necessary to make a profit from renting the cottage, since she derives considerable enjoyment from being able to use it herself as a base for the occasional week in the country.

Dales Cottage Holidays have informed her that a similar cottage two miles away brought

THE CROOKED MILE
SEDBUSK
NEAR HAWES
NORTH YORKSHIRE

* Accommodates 4 + baby
* Two well-behaved pets welcome
* Colour television + microwave
* Rent includes 2 storage heaters
* Garage and garden and sun lounge
* Peaceful position – lovely views

Sedbusk is an attractive, small Upper Dales village situated half-way up a Fell on the south-facing (and sunny) side of the broad sweeping valley of Wensleydale. Forming its backdrop this Fell climbs to over 2000ft, part craggy and part moorland at its summit. Served by a narrow, twisting and fairly steep road which comes to an abrupt halt at the end of the village there is no through traffic therefore and a peaceful, relaxing, almost sleepy atmosphere abounds. Indeed it is a typical Upper Dales village, self-contained, with about 25 houses, cottages and barns in total, dating mostly from the 18th and 19th century, and spread all higgledly-piggledly over its confines. Hardly any two doors face the same direction, a modern day planners' nightmare perhaps but for those who appreciate a more traditional and less regimented village development, bursting full of charm and character.

Sedbusk lies about 1 mile from the busy tourist centre of Hawes, a market town with full amenities and a range of shops, cafes, pubs and restaurants. As you turn the corner out of the village on the road to Hawes a view of real distinction unfolds over the beautiful valley of Wensleydale and the sharp-eyed observer will be able to follow the course of the River Ure as it flows down the Dale towards Aysgarth Falls. Footpaths criss-cross the Dale, including the Pennine Way which passes very close to Sedbusk and keen walkers will need little prompting to get out and enjoy the bracing Dales air. For the less energetic Sedbusk is an ideal base to tour the Yorkshire Dales, with Wharfedale and Swaledale close by, and the Lake District and North York Moors around 1 hour's easy drive away through marvellous scenery.

THE CROOKED MILE, SEDBUSK, WENSLEYDALE – *Occupying a lovely position overlooking the tiny village green in Sedbusk,* 'The Crooked Mile' is one of the very few recently built properties in the village. It is an appealing cottage and features the use of wall lights throughout which enhance its atmosphere and double aspect windows in most of the rooms with beautiful views over the surrounding upland pastures in which sheep and cows quietly graze. <u>*2 storage heaters (included in the rent) ensure a warm start for your holiday and background heat during your stay.*</u> Very tastefully decorated, furnished and carpeted throughout, *'The Crooked Mile' (the distance to Hawes along a delightful footpath through drystone walled meadows)* <u>presents this warm, very comfortable accommodation</u>:

<u>LOUNGE</u> with a comfortable settee and easy chairs, a colour TV and a storage heater. <u>DINING KITCHEN</u> with modern cupboards, ample work surface, an island bar with inset hob (2 rings), small oven/grill, *microwave*, toaster, fridge, *storage heater* and a pine dining table and 4 chairs. <u>SUN LOUNGE</u> with cane furniture and superb views over the upland pastures. <u>UPSTAIRS</u> – 2 ATTRACTIVE BEDROOMS (2 DOUBLES) *each with washbasins.* <u>SHOWER ROOM</u> with built-in cubicle and electric shower, washbasin and toilet. <u>OUTSIDE – GARAGE</u> with integral door off the kitchen. On site parking for 2 cars. Walled but not enclosed <u>GARDEN</u> laid to rough but regularly cut grass.

<u>SERVICES</u>: 2 *storage heaters* included in the rent. Various fixed and portable electric fires. Immersion heater. Electricity via £1 meter. *<u>Cot and high chair available on prior request.</u>* <u>LINEN</u>: There are ample blankets and pillows but *<u>you must bring your own sheets, pillowcases, towels, tea towels and a tablecloth.</u>* A linen hire service is available – Details on request.

in gross rent of £6750 in 1994, for 28 weeks' rental. Twenty-five per cent of this return was paid to Dales Cottage Holidays who acted as booking agents on her behalf.

She has worked out the costs of owning the cottage as follows:
- mortgage repayments: **£400 per month**
- electricity: **£15 per week** (while the property is occupied)
- oil for central heating: **£12 per week** (costed out throughout the year)
- business rates*: **£630 per year**
- insurance of the building and its contents: **£285 per year**
- water: **£63 per quarter**
- cleaning costs at changeover of tenants: **£12 per turn round** (including provision of consumables like toilet rolls, bin liners, light bulbs etc.).

* Business rates replace council tax because the property has a business use.

1 Prepare a financial statement showing the financial costs of the property to the owner on a month-by-month basis.

2 Collect two brochures produced by different companies offering country cottages for rent and discuss the range of prices quoted, and the factors which you think might account for the variations in price.

3 Suggest two pricing schedules for The Crooked Mile which indicate different price levels for the four seasons and two savers which form the basis of Dales Cottage Holidays' pricing structure:

   a) the first schedule should aim to maximise income

   b) the second schedule should aim to maximise occupation.

   In determining these price levels, you should take account of both the owner's costs and the price range quoted by other cottage holiday companies.

4.6 A business diversifying into tourism: The Teapottery

Develops knowledge and understanding of the following element:
4.2 Examine financial accounts in leisure and tourism organisations

Supports development of the following core skills:
Application of number 3.2, 3.3 (Task 1)
Application of number 3.3; Communication 3.4 (Task 2)
Application of number 3.2 (Task 3)
Application of number 3.2 (Task 4)
Application of number 3.2 (Task 5)

Judy and Martin Bibby set up their own ceramics business in Coverdale in 1979. They had developed their own style of eccentric ceramics and had starting selling these, largely through personal contacts. Initially they supplied two shops in Central London, Strangeways and Ideas, who would order on the basis of what they thought they could sell. In the early 1980s most high streets contained at least one small shop selling ceramics. However, the recession of the late 1980s resulted in the closure of many of these.

The establishment of the business was gradual. Finance was not available for what was then an operation that could not guarantee to be profitable. The Bibbys took other jobs in order to save for a kiln and initially worked from home. In financial terms they always worked within their own means. As orders increased, so working from home became more difficult. Commitments to supply customers had to be met on time, and this was hampered by limited space and by the fact that the house would occasionally get cut off by snow in the winter!

The company moved to Leyburn in 1983, initially on a four-year lease. Some contract work was taken on in order to provide some financial security. However orders for their own work increased sufficiently for the contract work to cease. In 1986 the business began to specialise in making teapots. In 1991 the premises were expanded and the Teapottery now employs 29 craftspeople producing over 30 lines for select retailers, with over 40 per cent of production currently going to export.

Expanding the business was achieved largely through increasing sales. New business is now acquired through two major trade shows held at the National Exhibition Centre – the International Spring Gift Fair in February and the International Autumn Gift Fair in September. Both of these events generate export orders to North America, Europe and the Far East. In financial terms, the timing of these events is interesting. The retail trade in ceramics will have certain times of the year when sales peak. The period between September and Christmas sees an increase in sales as people buy gifts. The time between February and Easter is important as shops go through the process of restocking after the January sales. Companies proposing to export ceramics from the Teapottery will test them early in the year, ready for export in July and September.

Developing a tourism aspect to the business has a particular advantage for the Teapottery. The peak interest from a tourism point of view is during the school summer holidays, at Easter, and during the spring and autumn half terms. In other words the tourism trade often provides cash for the business at times when the retail side of the business is not at its peak.

When the Teapottery premises were extended in 1991, there was enough space to provide a walkway for visitors, giving them a clear view of the making process. They can watch every stage of the teapot manufacturing process, from slip-casting to painting, glazing and firing. Informative printed labels provide an illustrated guide to each stage of the process.

The walkway leads from the factory to a shop where the finished products are on sale. One of the costs of any manufacturing process is the number of faulty products which appear. While every business would want to reduce the number of 'seconds' created, it is inevitable that there will be some. In ceramics these can be caused in a number of different ways:

- a pot may be dropped, chipped or broken
- a system fault may result in a paint spray gun failing to function properly
- bad firing in the kiln may damage a pot's finish
- the glaze may be applied too thickly to the pot.

The benefit of a shop is that 'seconds' can be sold rather than thrown away and so do not represent a total loss. They are clearly labelled as 'seconds', though the faults are often not very obvious, and sold at a reduced price. This acts as a kind of quality control, since it enables the company to ensure that only the highest quality goods are supplied to other retail outlets.

In 1995 the Bibbys opened a second Teapottery in Keswick. The established reputation and business record of the company meant that there was no problem in borrowing capital to help to set up this new outlet. The location, close to the centre of Keswick, is important in that it is in a popular tourism destination and is expected to attract a substantial number of visitors. Teapots are made and sold on the premises. The extra manufacturing capacity of these second premises should help the company to meet all its orders during the peak season.

A business which depends on selling a range of product lines will sometimes have to assess how well individual products are performing. The Teapottery will employ an accountant to cost a particular line. The costs of labour and materials are calculated, and added to a proportion of other costs such as heat, power and lighting. The total is related to variables such as the time taken to make the particular pot and the number being made in the batch.

Various kinds of financial records are kept in order to keep track of different aspects of the business. Sales in the shop are recorded in a Shop Book and an example of how this information is set out is given below.

Date	Non-VAT	ITEM	First or second	Drinks	Cash, CC, £ cheque	
25/5/95		2 coffees & biscuits		£2.04		
		Aga & veg stall	2/2		cheque	55.00
		2 tea infusers			cash	3.00
		Welsh dresser (one cup)	2		cash	16.00
		Fireside (one cup)	2		cash	16.00
		Fireside (one cup)	1		cheque	20.00
		Traveller (Orient Express)	2		CC	31.50
		2 teas & Eccles cakes		£2.16		
		Piano (one cup)	1		CC	20.00
		Welsh Dresser	2		cash	27.50
	£3.60	40 tea bags				3.60
		2 x Butchers block	2/2		CC	63.00
		Lilt, coffee & biscuit		£1.65		
		Miniature teapot	1		cash	3.50
		Bellhop & statue	1/2		CC	49.50
		Wheelbarrow	1		cheque	38.50
		2 teas		£1.20		
		Woodburner & TV	1/2		CC	44.00
		2 x Bellhop	1/1		CC	66.00
	£3.60	40 tea bags				3.60
		Wheelbarrow	1		cheque	38.50
		Paul Cardew figure	1		CC	60.00
	£7.20		TOTALS	£7.05		559.20

566.25

Your tasks

Study the Shop Book extract and then answer the following questions.

1 Do firsts or seconds generate more cash in the shop?

2 What is the purpose of the non-VAT column in the book?

3 If there was a £20 cash float in the till at the beginning of the day, how much cash should there be in the till at the end of the day?

4 Assume that the shop is open six days a week and that the average daily takings over the whole year are 70 per cent of the amount taken on 25 May. What is the annual turnover in the shop?

5 Calculate the amount of credit card business which the shop did during the day. Assume that they have to pay a 4 per cent merchant charge to the banks in order to be able to offer credit card services. If this charge is deducted before the shop seeks payment from the credit card companies, how much will the shop actually claim?

4.7 Preparing a promotional budget for Granada Studios Tour

Develops knowledge and understanding of the following element:
4.3 Investigate and carry out simple budgeting in leisure and tourism

Supports development of the following core skills:
Application of number 3.2, 3.3; Communication 3.4; Information Technology 3.3 (Task 1)
Application of number 3.3; Communication 3.2 (Task 2)

Granada Studios Tour was opened as a tourist attraction in 1988, largely as a response to the many requests from the public wanting a 'behind the scenes' view of television and film production. The main intention of the attraction was to provide visitors with first-hand experience of how films and television programmes are put together. While a backstage tour is a focal point for the whole experience, there is a range of other attractions on the site.

Granada Studios tour attractions

1 **Backstage tour** – a 30-minute guided tour looking at costumes, props, make-up, continuity, camera work and set design
2 **Soundstage Tour** – a 30-minute tour looking at special effects, stage sets and special lighting effects
3 **The Baker Street Victorian Extravaganza** – a film set of a Victorian London street, complete with shops, a Sherlock Holmes Museum and regular Old Time Music Hall shows

4 **The Coronation Street Experience** – the open air set of the famous TV drama, including well-known landmarks like The Rover's Return

5 **The Sound Effects Show** – a 30-minute show illustrating the problems faced by sound engineers and showing how they resolve them

6 **The House of Commons Debate** – a replica film set of the House of Commons is the location for a light-hearted series of parliamentary debates with plenty of opportunities for audience participation

7 **The Sooty Show** – a 20-minute show for younger children featuring the well-known television puppet

8 **Downtown New York** – a new York street set with yellow taxi cabs and uniformed police officers

9 **The UFO Zone** – a continuous ride simulating the consequences of an alien spacecraft landing at Granada Studios Tour

10 **Robocop: the Rid**e – a futuristic simulator ride featuring Robocop's pursuit of a group of kidnappers

11 **Haunts of the Olde Country** – a 20-minute 3-D presentation featuring an American tourist's encounters with a series of ghosts

12 **The 3-D Rock Laser Show** – a 15-minute light and laser show featuring a range of current popular rock music

13 **The Deadly Effects Show** – a 30-minute show illustrating some of the special effects used in horror films

14 **Coronation Street Studio Sets** – interior sets featuring houses and workplaces of well-known characters

From time to time Granada Studios Tour will plan promotions. The main purpose of these is usually to attract a greater volume of sales, but they may also be used to try and develop the public image of what the attraction has to offer. Promotions are generally classified as either strategic or tactical:

Type of promotion	Time span	Objectives
Strategic promotion	Long term	Intended to build up the brand image or communicate major changes such as new opening times
Tactical promotion	Short term	Often used to launch a new attraction and intended to increase revenue at off peak periods

The budget for a promotion will relate both to the length of time it is to run, and also to the type of approach and media to be used. For example, a promotion might use television, national or regional press, posters or direct mail, or any combination of these. It could also be launched jointly with the manufacturer of a retail product likely to appeal to a similar market.

The first step in planning the promotion is to establish objectives. These may be measurable targets, such as expanding sales volume by 10 per cent during the period of the promotion. They may also be related to qualitative issues, such as changing the public perception of the attraction. The latter example is particularly relevant for Granada Studios Tour since many people associate it solely with *Coronation Street* and are unaware of the range of different attractions on the site.

The budget for a promotion will have to cover a wide range of costs. These will include paying fees or salaries to the people who are going to create the promotion. For example, if

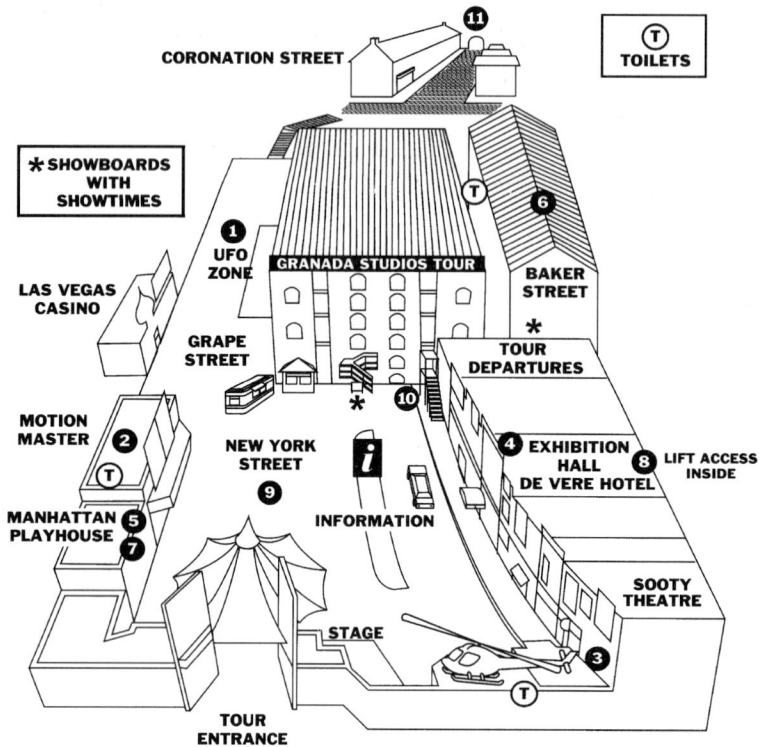

CORONATION STREET

⑪

Ⓣ TOILETS

*SHOWBOARDS WITH SHOWTIMES

① UFO ZONE

GRANADA STUDIOS TOUR

Ⓣ

⑥

BAKER STREET

LAS VEGAS CASINO

GRAPE STREET

* TOUR DEPARTURES

*

⑩

MOTION MASTER ②

Ⓣ

NEW YORK STREET

ℹ

④ EXHIBITION HALL DE VERE HOTEL

⑧ LIFT ACCESS INSIDE

MANHATTAN PLAYHOUSE ⑤ ⑦

⑨

INFORMATION

SOOTY THEATRE

STAGE

③

Ⓣ

TOUR ENTRANCE

Key

1 The UFO Zone
2 Robocop: the Ride
3 The Sooty Show
4 The House of Commons Debate
5 The Deadly Effects Show
6 The Baker Street set
7 The Sound Effects Show
8 The 3-D Rock Laser Show
9 Downtown New York
10 The Backstage Tour
11 Coronation Street

television coverage is felt to be appropriate, designing and making the advertisement requires a number of specialist skills. Leaflets and posters require specialist design, art-work, printing and distribution input, and this work will often be handled by external agencies.

Promotions often incorporate a factor which will enable their effects to be accurately monitored. For example reduced admission rates might be offered, a prize draw might be launched, tokens might be issued on other products to be redeemed at the attraction or free gifts could be made available. The budget will have to incorporate the costs of offering any of these incentives.

Promotions need a target audience if they are to be cost-effective. Granada Studios Tour receives some 350,000 group visitors each year. These groups fall into three main categories.

1 **Operators** – visitors arriving in pre-booked coach parties organised by tour operators or coach companies. These make up 40 per cent of the total number of group admissions. Their incentive to visit is financial, since the companies will receive discounts if they increase the amount of business they bring to Granada Studios Tour.

2 **Directs** – visitors arriving on independently organised trips, such as those run by social clubs. They account for 40 per cent of visitors and their motivation to visit is primarily the interests of the group.

3 **School parties** – pre-booked school groups, representing 20 per cent of all visitors. Their purpose may be to have a fun day out, but increasingly such visits have under-lying educational objectives relating to the school curriculum.

A promotion intended to increase the number of visits by any one of these group types needs to take account of the prevailing economic circumstances. Disposable income has not increased much in the last two years, and factors like inflation and the reduction of coach speed limits to 60 m.p.h. may combine to increase the cost operators charge to arrange coach tours.

Your tasks

Below are some cost indicators for different methods of promoting Granada Studios Tour to coach operators and independent group organisers.

Direct mail (administration and distribution): £450 per 1000 items
Brochure design: Design of 4-colour 12-page brochure = £5000
Printing of this brochure = £8000 per 10 000 copies
Field sales: £400 per week for 20 appointments (petrol and salary)
Telephone sales: £3.50 per hour
Trade press advertising:

Journal	full page colour	half page colour
Group Travel Organiser	£1100	£650
Coach Tours UK	£900	£450
Coach and Bus Week	£1000	£550
Coaching Journal	£1050	£500

Artwork costs £750 per advert

You are given the task of producing a breakdown of how a promotional budget of £100 000 should be spent. There are two objectives underlying this promotion:
  1 to increase the number of coach visits to Granada Studios Tour by 30 per cent
  2 to promote the attraction as a balanced family product, not just appealing to Coronation Street fans.

  1 Draw up your budget proposal.
  2 Write accompanying notes, describing why you allocated specific funds to different areas and explaining what you hope each expenditure will achieve.

4.8 Managing funds in a professional football club

Develops knowledge and understanding of the following element:
4.3 Investigate and carry out simple budgeting in leisure and tourism

Supports development of the following core skills:
Communication 3.2, 3.4 (Task 1)
Application of number 3.1; Communication 3.2 (Task 2)
Application of number 3.1, 3.2, 3.3 (Task 3)
Application of number 3.2; Communication 3.2 (Task 4)

All leisure facilities have to keep a record of their income and expenditure. Each year they prepare a budget, predicting how much they think they will receive from different sources and proposing how this income should be spent. They then monitor this process throughout the year to ensure that they are meeting their expected income targets and not exceeding their planned spending. Unexpected rises or falls in income or expenditure will generally result in adjustments having to be made to the original budget plans.

Facilities where a number of activities take place need more careful analysis of income and expenditure. An arts centre may find that its weekly film shows are very popular and therefore profitable, but its theatre performances are more costly to put on and are attracting very small audiences. The centre will have to balance what its policy says about providing a variety of arts experiences against its need not to show large losses. In other words, showing more films and fewer plays might be more profitable, but might also cater for a smaller section of the local community.

Swindon Town Football Club

Like most professional football clubs Swindon Town derives its income from a variety of sources. These are:

- gate receipts
- programme sales
- sponsorship
- fees from the Football League
- hire charges for function rooms
- sales of goods in the club shop
- profits from catering and drinks sales at the ground.

Gate receipts form an important part of the club's income. However, it is not easy to predict the level of this income since it will vary considerably. Fewer supporters may turn up in bad weather or if the opposition is not regarded as a very attractive team. The major factor which determines attendance is the current form of the home team. How well they are playing, which division they are in and whether they have a good run in any of the Cup competitions will all affect the size of the crowds they attract.

Most clubs calculate at the beginning of each season what size their average crowd needs to be if they are to meet all their costs. In the 1991–2 season Swindon needed an average gate of 11 500. Promotion to the Premier League meant increased costs in order to make necessary ground improvements. The average attendance required to meet these increased costs became 14 500. The requirement that the ground be an all-seater stadium by the start of the 1994–5 season has reduced its current capacity to 18 500, a disadvantage if the club should be drawn at home in a Cup game against one of the big Premier League teams.

The sales of season tickets are particularly of interest. These provide much needed income at the beginning of the season. More importantly, they are guaranteed receipts, regardless of the team's performance during the season.

Sponsorship is also important to the club, though it takes a number of different forms. The main sponsor, on a three-year contract with the club, is Burmah Oil. In return for a fixed annual contribution, the company's logo is carried around the ground, and on club kit and merchandising items.

Various other kinds of sponsorship are also in operation. A number of executive suites are sponsored by local companies. This enables them to bring up to 20 guests to each match, and includes the provision of refreshments before and after the game. Advertising boards around the ground are sold for a set fee each season. Some of these can be picked up by television cameras and Lucozade, one of the companies using these boards, pay the club a bonus each time a Lucozade advertisement is picked up by TV cameras filming a Swindon home match.

Other smaller sponsorship deals are also available. Individual games can be sponsored, which provide the sponsor's guests with a meal, a tour of the ground, a meeting with the players and the manager, and photographs to mark the occasion. Individuals can sponsor different items of a player's kit or the match ball for a specific game.

In addition to the usual sources of income Swindon Town also raises money from a variety of fund-raising events. These include activities like lotteries, scratch card schemes, bingo, fashion shows, and evening social events such as dinner dances and karaoke nights.

Sponsorship, like gate receipts, is affected by the club's position in the League. The more successful the team's performance on the field, the easier it is to attract sponsors and people wishing to hire function rooms. If the club is not matching its targets in terms of sponsorship and gate receipts, it affects cash flow. With more money going out in costs than coming in in revenue, the club will be obliged to cut costs by reducing administration or staff, or by selling players. On the other hand, exceeding targets may allow the club to purchase new players or invest money in improving the ground facilities.

Fuller details of the various sponsorship arrangements at the club are provided on pages 108 and 109.

Your tasks

1 Draw up a list of budget headings suitable for use by the financial manager of a professional football club.

2 List the main expenses which you think Swindon Town Football Club will have to meet in the coming season. Undertake sufficient research to enable you to provide rough estimates of each of these costs.

3 Draw up a budget estimating the club's income from different sources for the coming season and setting this against your estimated costs.

4 Write a general report indicating what implications each of the following will have on your budget plans:
   - attendances fall below predicted levels
   - the club has a successful run in the FA Cup
   - there is a fire in the club shop
   - the main sponsor offers to extend its contract with the club for a further two years, while at the same time raising its fixed annual contribution by 10 per cent
   - a supermarket chain offers to buy land owned by the club for £10 million.

Swindon Town Football Club Business Opportunities 1994/5 Season

MATCH KIT SPONSORSHIP

A very popular method of showing your support and at the same time bringing your Company's name or product to a wide audience. Sponsor your favourite player's kit for the season and in return you will receive an acknowledgment in every match day programme, including cup games.

Choose your player's shirt, shorts, socks, boots, tracksuit or training shoes, or better still, his entire kit.

Costs				
	Whole kit	£330	Shorts	£90
	Tracksuit	£75	Socks	£35
	Training shoes	£60	Match boots	£75
	Shirt	£90		

MATCHDAY SPONSORSHIP

Matchday Sponsorship offers a very powerful package of benefits that enables your Company to maximise on a very wide range of promotion and hospitality opportunities.

As always, our professional marketing team ensure that your day is a total success from the morning reception right through to the post-match presentation.

The Matchday Sponsorship Package includes:

- A drinks reception on arrival
- A 'Behind the Scenes' tour of the County Ground
- A superb 4-course meal with wine
- Half-time refreshments of tea, coffee and biscuits
- Full-time refreshments including post-match buffet
- Executive box seats
- Complimentary matchday programmes for your guests
- Front cover flash on matchday programme
- STFC gift pack for each guest
- Two Director's car park passes
- The opportunity for your guests to vote for the 'Man of the Match' and make the award to the player after the game
- Photo opportunities of your 'Man of the Match' presentation
- Photo opportunities for your group with members of the squad
- Business card raffle
- Autographed football for 'Guest of the Day'
- An advertisement in the matchday programme
- An editorial write up in the programme
- An acknowledgement on the public address system

Costs	Category	A	B	C
	40 guests	£4,500	£4,000	£3,500
	20 guests	£2,500	£2,250	£2,000

SPONSOR A GOAL

This is a new and exciting opportunity to have your name appear in every home matchday programme. So put your money where your mouth is by sponsoring £5, £2, or £1 for each LEAGUE GOAL scored.

To give you an idea of what your commitment could be Swindon Town have scored 47, 69 and 74 goals during each of the last three seasons.

MATCH BALL SPONSORSHIP

One of the most popular of all the schemes at Swindon Town Football Club. This package presents a high profile for your Company on a specific match day, all at a relatively low cost.

Your package for four includes:

- Executive Box seats for 6 people
- An autographed football presented by a member of the STFC squad
- A 'Behind the Scenes' tour of the County Ground
- Table reservations and pre-match buffet in our Executive Suite
- Complimentary drink on arrival
- Complimentary half-time refreshments
- Post-match access to Executive Suite
- Complimentary matchday programme and STFC gift pack for each guest
- Your own hostess for the day
- An advertisement in the matchday programme and on the Public Address system prior to the match

The matches are graded A,B and C and the price of the Match Ball sponsorship varies according to the grade of the game.

Costs	Category	A	B	C
		£500	£450	£400

MATCH DAY MASCOT

It's every young supporters dream to become a mascot, to meet and to run onto the pitch with their favourite team for the home fixture of their choice.

Before leading the teams out onto the pitch for the pre-match warm up and photograph, one of our matchday staff will conduct the mascots on a 'Behind the Scenes' guided tour of the ground.

Why not make it a family occasion and bring your grand-parents, aunts, uncles or even your friends to share in this wonderful experience. Additional match tickets, hospitality lounge passes and pre-match buffets are available on request.

The Matchday Mascot package includes:

- Three complimentary match tickets (including mascot's)
- Three passes for the hospitality lounge
- A 'Behind the Scenes' guided tour of the ground
- Pre-match buffet for three
- Meet the STFC Players, Manager and Coaching staff
- A full replica STFC kit
- A visit to the home dressing room
- A pre-match warm up on the pitch with the team
- Lead the team out for the game
- A souvenir photo with both team Captains and matchday officials
- A photo and an editorial piece in the matchday programme
- Automatic membership to the 'Junior Robins' supporters club
- A STFC gift pack
- Complimentary matchday programme

Costs	
	£200 plus VAT

PERIMETER ADVERTISING

A hard hitting, full colour ground board, seen by an average of 10,000 live spectators at least once a fortnight is only the start of the story. The visual impact of these colourful boards is also seen as a backdrop to many photographs taken at matches by professional photographers on assignment for soccer magazines, local and national press and, of course, the Club Programme.

TV sites as indicated below, will be guaranteed exposure at every game played at the County Ground throughout the season, including Anglo Italian, Coca-Cola and FA Cup matches and all live broadcasts and recorded highlights.

The Club's signwriter is available to assist you with the design and production of your board or you can supply your own sign to our specification.

Costs	North Stand	A1-A15 (TV)	£2,500
	Town End	B1-B11 (TV)	£2,500
	Stratton Bank	C1-C11 (TV)	£2,500
	Upper Stratton Bank	C12-C21 (TV)	£2,000
	Intel Stand	D1-D15	£1,400
	Upper Intel Stand	D16-D30	£1,200

EXECUTIVE MEMBERSHIP

The Executive Suite is an ideal venue for Company entertaining with a relaxed atmosphere all of it's own. Executive membership is limited to around 120 people, all of whom will have matchday access to the exclusive facilities of the Executive lounge and bar, which are second to none.

The Executive Membership includes the following:

- Executive Box seats for all league and cup matches
- Complimentary matchday programme
- Two course quality hot buffet
- Licensed bar facilities
- Half-time refreshments
- Sky TV sports coverage
- Free admission to reserve matches
- Priority bookings on Executive away trips
- Discounted rates on the hire of our function facilities for parties, weddings, conferences, special events etc, subject to availability
- An exclusive Executive Members pin badge
- Monthly Executive news letter (full members only)

Costs	Executive Membership per season	£1000
	Executive Membership per season renewal	£850
	Executive Day Membership	£50

PROGRAMME ADVERTISING

Swindon Town's bright, colourful and informative Matchday Magazine is widely acknowledged as one of the best in the business. This publication is on sale at all home matches played at the County Ground and is often treasured as a collectors item with a readership way beyond its 180,000 plus sales. Colour spaces are available on a full season basis. The high quality of the editorial content means that the space available for programme advertising is at a premium and we recommend that any enquiries be submitted as early as possible.

SPORTING DINNERS & SPECIAL EVENTS

If you are looking to host a corporate event with a difference, especially one with a sporting theme, STFC can offer a wealth of ideas, together with the necessary expertise and experience in organising and executing such occasions.

For example, one of our most successful innovations with local companies has been a series of Sporting Dinners held throughout the year. These offer an excellent blend of corporate hospitality and entertainment. The evening begins with a superb 4-course meal followed by two after-dinner guest speakers. The first is from the world of sport and the second is usually a well known comedian or public speaker.

The evening provides an ideal opportunity to entertain business clients, friends and associates as well as giving you a unique chance to deliver a Company message to a relaxed yet captive audience.

The Sporting Dinner sponsorship includes:

- Champagne reception in private with after dinner speaker and members of Swindon Town Football Club
- Complimentary table of ten
- Place on top table for main member of party
- Mention of Company Sponsorship on menu
- Photograph of group taken with celebrity and guest speaker

If you prefer to entertain your guests 'al fresco' STFC is equally experienced in organising outdoor events.

Again, an excellent example is our popular Golf Day, where guests may have the opportunity to tee off with players from the team.

These events can be customised to suit your needs and could include a welcoming package, lunch, 18 holes of quality golf with a Cannon start, competitions and prizes. All followed by an excellent meal and after dinner speakers.

We welcome enquiries on every aspect of corporate entertaining and invite you to discuss your requirements with our Marketing Team on 0793 430430.

Main Sponsor Burmah

Following a highly successful 3-season debut as Main Sponsor to Swindon Town Football Club, Burmah Petroleum Fuels Limited have renewed their commitment for a further 3 years.

Burmah Petroleum Fuels Limited, who were voted 'Oil Company of the Year, 1993' is a major division of Burmah Castrol Plc and the largest independent wholesaler in the UK with a network of 1,300 sites.

The only petrol company to sponsor our National sport at top level, Burmah regards its STFC involvement as a major part of its marketing and promotional mix and has created and implemented a comprehensive pro-active programme of events in addition to utilising the sponsorship in media advertising.

For everyone associated with Swindon Town Football Club, from the Chairman to the last supporter through the gates on a Saturday, the involvement of a major petrol Company as a main sponsor creates a feeling of security and confidence which can only reflect favourably on all participants.

Glossary

base rate the rate which banks use to determine the interest they will charge to borrowers

bequests sums of money or property left in a will to another person or organisation

bond a sum of money held on behalf of a company, to be used to refund their customers should the company go out of business

branding using a name or trade mark to make individual products easy to distinguish from their competitors, and to establish them in the minds of existing and potential customers

capital works major fixed investment usually associated with buildings or equipment and often funded by long term loans or directly out of company profits

cash flow the movement of money received and paid out by a business

charitable trust a non-profit-making organisation overseeing the use of funds often donated specifically for the upkeep and management of property or estates

compulsory competitive tendering (CCT) a requirement of the Local Government Act (1988) setting up a process by which some local authority services, such as leisure provision, have to be defined in a contract for which private companies wishing to manage these services can compete

contingency plan a plan made in order to be ready for the occurrence of some chance or unexpected situation

crime audit a detailed assessment of the crime risks in a specific location and the remedial actions which these might require

deeds of covenant legal agreements usually covering a set period and often involving the contribution of funds to another person or organisation

directives decisions passed on as instructions from one organisation having authority over others

documentation all the written paperwork which supports a business transaction

endowment money which is settled on a specific property in order to maintain and restore it

English Tourist Board a national government-funded organisation aiming to encourage the British to take more holidays in England and to improve the facilities available to them when they do

ethos the type of behaviour and atmosphere which is characteristic of an organisation

freehold property which the owner is free to dispose of or pass on as an inheritance

heritage sites, buildings and artefacts reflecting the achievements and way of life of our ancestors

job description a statement of the duties and responsibilities which the holder of a specific job is expected to carry out

legacy money or personal property left in a will

liability	responsibility to protect clients against risk
logo	a symbol, picture or design used to identify a company or product
market value	the current price which potential purchasers are willing to pay for goods or services
media	means by which information is passed on to the public, for example newspapers, radio, television
networked	linked into a system of computer terminals which can pass information to one another
occupancy rate	a means of measuring how successfully hotels are performing by calculating the percentage of rooms occupied and whether each of these is a single or double occupancy
person specification	a description of the skills and qualities expected of suitable recruits for an advertised job
premium payment	a single sum of money paid for insurance
private sector	businesses owned and operated by private individuals and firms
privatise	to convert a business or organisation from government funding to private ownership
pro forma	a document or form in which the layout and wording has been standardised
public sector	organisations and businesses financed by government funds
regeneration	the rebuilding and revitalising of areas such as city centres
remortgage	borrowing an additional sum of money using the increased value of property as security
retail travel	the process of selling travel arrangements directly to customers
security	land or property offered as a guarantee against the repayment of a loan
source markets	the area from which potential customers are derived
subsidiary	a less important branch of a company, but one which contributes to their overall profit
tagging	a system of using labels attached to goods which set off an alarm if they are removed from the premises
target markets	the consumer groups to which a company is aiming to sell its products and services
Tourist Information Centre	a centre providing information about transport, accommodation and attractions in the surrounding area
turnover	the money value of a company's total sales and other income over a specified period
viability	the likelihood of a business or scheme being successful
voluntary sector	organisations funded by members, voluntary contributions and charities